FIFTH PLANET AND OTHER PLAYS

BY DAVID AUBURN

★

★

DRAMATISTS
PLAY SERVICE
INC.

To Carl Forsman

CONTENTS

FIFTH PLANET

FIFTH PLANET was first produced at the New York Stage and Film Festival in Poughkeepsie, New York, on July 17, 1995. It was directed by Lizzie Gottlieb. The cast was as follows:

VERONICA .... Christina Kirk
MIKE .... Tim Guinee

Note: This play has 44 short scenes. Each scene is a different night. Props can be set as needed in the blackouts, which should be quick: some could last no more than a second. There are no set changes, and the actors can wear the same clothes throughout, except for the coats for different weather, as indicated.

FIFTH PLANET

Scene 1

The top of a hill. The sun sets. The sky above the hill fills with stars. Mike enters, crossing. He stops, transfixed by the sight. Blackout.

Scene 2

Stars. Mike enters. He wears a workman's jumpsuit, keys dangling from his belt. He removes it, street clothes underneath. Takes a beer out of his pocket, pops it open. Sits, drinks, watches the sky. Fade.

Scene 3

Mike now has a telescope set up on a tripod. He looks through it in wonder, scanning. Veronica enters, crossing. When she crosses Mike's line of sight Mike jumps, startled. She smiles politely. Mike regards her, an animal guarding his territory. She retreats. Fade. Pause.

Scene 4

Mike and telescope. Veronica enters, walking straight across the stage.

VERONICA. *(Calling.)* I'm on my way to work!
MIKE. Thank you! *(Blackout.)*

Scene 5

Mike and telescope. Veronica enters, snorts.

MIKE. What?
VERONICA. Nothing.
MIKE. What is it? *(She exits swiftly. Mike stammers.)* What — *(She is gone. Blackout.)*

Scene 6

Mike in the same position. Veronica enters.

MIKE. *(Instantly.)* What?
VERONICA. Nothing. *(Blackout.)*

Scene 7

Same position. Veronica enters, crossing.

MIKE. Hi. *(She keeps walking.)* Please.
VERONICA. What?
MIKE. Come on.
VERONICA. *What?*
MIKE. Before. A week, two weeks ago. What is it?
VERONICA. What is what?
MIKE. You were laughing. You laughed. *(Beat.)*
VERONICA. *(Indicates telescope.)* What do you do with that?
MIKE. Look at the sky.
VERONICA. At what?
MIKE. Stars.
VERONICA. Which ones?
MIKE. See that big orange star?
VERONICA. Uh huh.
MIKE. That's Jupiter.
VERONICA. Jupiter is a *planet.*
MIKE. I know. It looks like a star from here. I meant —
VERONICA. It looks like a star because you've got a little telescope. *(Blackout.)*

Scene 8

Mike in the same position. Veronica enters.

VERONICA.   *(Crossing.)* And that's not Jupiter. *(She exits. Blackout.)*

11

Scene 9

Mike and the telescope. He has a large reference book.

MIKE. Jupiter. Fifth planet from the sun. It is the largest and most massive planet in the solar system. *(He searches for it. No luck.)* It's the largest and most massive fucking planet in the solar system. *(Blackout.)*

Scene 10

Mike and the telescope. Veronica enters. Mike doesn't see her. Mike is looking around blindly, as before. Beat. Then Veronica abruptly swivels the telescope, startling Mike. She repositions it. He glares at her, then stares though the eyepiece.

MIKE. *(Pleased.)* Hey! *(Veronica exits. Blackout.)*

Scene 11

Mike and Veronica.

VERONICA. *(Indicating telescope.)* May I?
MIKE. Well. All right.
VERONICA. Thanks. *(She walks over and looks through the eyepiece.)* Oooh! *(Laughs.)*
MIKE. *(Touchy.)* What?
VERONICA. Nothing. It's very. You're really got the ... could I

make a few suggestions?

MIKE. What?

VERONICA. Well, let's see. *(She tightens the telescope on the tripod, cleans the lens and the eyepiece and makes a few other little improvements.)* This is a lot like my first telescope, which I bought when I was thirteen. Saturn's rings, mountains on the moon, Jupiter of course, the binary in Orion — I did all the teen faves. There. *(Mike looks through the telescope.)*

MIKE. *(Surprised.)* Hey.

VERONICA. Good night. *(Veronica exits. Mike is glued to the eyepiece. Blackout.)*

Scene 12

Veronica addresses Mike.

VERONICA. Jupiter. Fifth planet from the sun. It is both the largest and the most massive of the planets. Ancient astronomers had no knowledge of the relative sizes of the planets, of course. But they were lucky and they picked the right name: Jupiter. King of the gods. There are sixteen known satellites, though we're hoping that figure will change soon, and then change again. It is the only planet other than the Earth known to have a magnetic field. The violent, surging atmosphere, of which the famous "Red Spot" — big enough to hold 100 earths — is the most prominent feature, is composed primarily of methane, ammonia, and hydrogen. *(Blackout.)*

Scene 13

Veronica's lecture continues. Mike is looking a little impatient.

VERONICA. Galileo was the first to see Jupiter's four largest moons: Io, Europa, Ganymede, and Callisto. He was using one of the very first telescopes, which, however, was slightly more sophisticated than the one you have. Io, Europa, Ganymede, Callisto. Beautiful names! The first objects discovered by a human using a telescope! Oh, this is interesting, and you probably don't know it: sixty-five years later. A Danish astronomer called Ole Romer noticed a discrepancy between the predicted times of the moons' eclipses and the observed times. And he explained the discrepancy by — guesses? No. No. Okay, I'll tell you: by positing a finite velocity for the propagation of light! Io, Europa, Ganymede and Callisto led us straight to the most fundamental fact in science!
MIKE. You know a lot about Jupiter.
VERONICA. Mm-hm.
MIKE. You work up at the observatory.
VERONICA. Yes. We have a very big telescope. *(She exits. Blackout.)*

Scene 14

Veronica enters. Mike is looking through his telescope.

VERONICA. How is it?
MIKE. Fine. I don't need another lecture.
VERONICA. I don't want to have to give you one.
MIKE. I usually come here to be alone for a few hours after work. I don't mean to be —

VERONICA. I used to come here for the same thing before work.
MIKE. Uh huh. Well you've got a whole observatory. This is all I have. *(Beat. Then, exploding:)* I can't see a fucking thing through this. *(Beat.)*
VERONICA. It's cloudy tonight. *(Beat.)* It's usually fairly difficult to see any stars under those conditions. It's one of those things you pick up in grad school. *(She exits. Blackout.)*

Scene 15

Veronica alone.

VERONICA. People say, what do you do on rainy nights? When it's overcast, you can't see anything. *(She laughs.)* But observation's just a small part of what we do. Rainy nights are the best nights, Dr. Ayers says. Rainy nights are when the thinking gets done. Dr. Ayers says that rainy nights are the most fun. *(Blackout.)*

Scene 16

Mike. Veronica crosses.

VERONICA. Hello.
MIKE. Hello.
VERONICA. I haven't seen you for a few nights.
MIKE. It's been raining.
VERONICA. Good. You're doing well. *(Blackout.)*

Scene 17

Mike. Veronica enters, stops.

VERONICA. Where's your telescope?
MIKE. Home. It's getting dark later now. I can't stay out all night.
VERONICA. Oh yes. That's called the "summer." *(Blackout.)*

Scene 18

Mike addresses us.

MIKE. I had a good time last night. Kiki — that's my wife — Kiki went out after work and rented us a movie and we had dinner on the couch and just watched together, you know. She got her favorite movie. She's probably seen it a hundred times. It's an old movie from the forties called *Triggerhappy* and it's about these ranchers in Nevada during the Gold Rush who hike up this mountain where they think there's going to be gold that they can mine. That's about the first third of the film right there, getting up the mountain and meeting the characters — there's the head cowboy or rancher, I can't remember who he is but his wife is Esther Williams, and there's an old prospector character who's Lionel Barrymore and a kid played by Mickey Rooney, and the cook on the wagon is Bill "Bojangles" Robinson. (I wouldn't remember all this except we have seen this movie about a hundred times.) So they get to the top of the mountain and there's a blizzard and everyone freezes their asses off. *And,* there's no gold. The picture gets kind of slow there. But then they go over the ridge and they find a natural amphitheater that's been carved into the rock by a glacier. So it's perfect for putting on shows. Everyone has an act.

The cowboy — *(Remembering.)* Joel McCrea! He's Joel McCrea — does rope tricks and Mickey Rooney tells jokes and sings, and Bill "Bojangles" Robinson tap dances, and the climax of the movie is an avalanche and the amphitheater is completely filled with snow. Then the sun comes out and it all melts. So Esther Williams — *pop!* Under her buckskins she's got her swimsuit on, and she and this all-girl rodeo troupe they met going up the hill, they dive in in formation. Kiki *loves* it. *(Blackout.)*

Scene 19

Mike alone, looking through the telescope.

MIKE. Hi Kiki. She fell asleep in front of the television and now it's playing snow. She's going to sleep till morning. It's clear and I can stay out all night. *(Blackout.)*

Scene 20

VERONICA. How's Jupiter?
MIKE. Fine.
VERONICA. You're finding it okay.
MIKE. Yeah. No problems.
VERONICA. It's not only the largest but also the most massive of the planets.
MIKE. Right. *(Beat.)* Is that what you do? Jupiter? Or —
VERONICA. Oh, yes. But, uh, actually we're very excited: we launched a probe seven years ago. Dr. Ayers and I have been consulting on it. And it will be orbiting Jupiter in a matter of weeks. So it's almost as though, what's the point of looking into a *telescope* now ...
MIKE. Right ...
VERONICA. When after seven years we'll actually be *in* the

17

Jovian system.

MIKE. Seven years. Wow.

VERONICA. It takes time to get there. Even light takes about twenty-eight minutes to get here from Jupiter.

MIKE. Huh.

VERONICA. Dr. Ayers will be in charge of the monitoring team. He's brilliant.

MIKE. Well you must be brilliant too.

VERONICA. Yes. *(Beat.)* I'm Dr. Babcock.

MIKE. Yes.

VERONICA. We've been working together for years. We have a very close working relationship. It's rare.

MIKE. That sounds good.

VERONICA. He's really very brilliant. *(Blackout.)*

Scene 21

Veronica addresses us.

VERONICA. You can sit on the earth looking at something until the Universe implodes but it's not necessarily going to get you any-where. You've got to get *up* there. "Up," well. Out. Unmanned exploration as a practical concept has been around at least since Tombaugh. (He discovered Pluto.) But Doctor Ayers — *Hans* — really rammed this one through. Championed it. *(Laughs.)* I remember the first night we — well, Dr. Ayers and I were on and we had had a run of nights of the most optimal viewing conditions you can imagine, it must have lasted three weeks, and we were there together every night. And of course we had plenty of time to talk. Dr. Ayers would say, "Get me the Windex, Dr. Babcock, I've fogged up the eyepiece again." And I'd go get it. Dr. Ayers breathes very hard. He's a very intense person. *(Faster.)* And one night, I remember it was about four a.m. on February nineteenth eleven years ago, I said, I was just casually talking, you know, I was just rambling and I said something on the order of, "an unmanned

Jovian orbital observation device could be in system within the decade if we obtained an '86 launch window." Or words to that effect. And I didn't really think Dr. Ayers was paying attention but before I knew it, he was in Houston. The next week.

And we were off and running. *(Blackout.)*

Scene 22

Mike and Veronica.

MIKE. How do you know if you've seen something new?
VERONICA. Ha. The Holy Grail.
MIKE. There are thousands of things up there.
VERONICA. Thousands?
MIKE. Millions.
VERONICA. You can't count the number of objects in the universe. Even asking the question is silly.
MIKE. But that you can *see*.
VERONICA. That I can see or that you can see?
MIKE. Okay, me.
VERONICA. You could sit here for twenty years and perhaps begin to approach counting the number of objects visible to you with this telescope. It would require a degree of dedication.
MIKE. How would you know if you've seen something that no one has ever seen before?
VERONICA. Don't worry.
MIKE. I'm not "worried."
VERONICA. You can't possibly. A serious observation, the kind that produces a new catagorizable object, let's say a comet, would take you at least a year. You have to have a pretty good idea what it is to keep track of it. And you have to track it to know what it really is.
MIKE. So it's impossible.
VERONICA. Not *impossible*. It happens. But you have to have graduate school. *(Blackout.)*

19

Scene 23

Mike looks through the telescope.

MIKE. Jupiter. Fifth planet from the sun. Largest and most massive. I am tracking it. I've got a book and I'm testing myself on where it will appear next. *(Swivels.)* Kiki. My wife. She turns out all the lights in the house so she can watch TV sitting in the blue glow. Kiki looks blue from here. Jupiter is orange. *(Blackout.)*

Scene 24

Mike. Veronica blows by.

MIKE. Doctor.
VERONICA. I can't talk. *(Blackout.)*

Scene 25

Mike and Veronica.

MIKE. Haven't seen you for a while.
VERONICA. Don't get me started.
MIKE. Okay …
VERONICA. For one thing I had to go in the last two *days*, which I *hate*.
MIKE. Why?
VERONICA. Ha-ha. In this business (it's not a business) in this

profession we depend on a lot of people — there's a large support staff and they're not always very knowledgeable. They're often very *stupid* and they have responsibility for some extraordinarily expensive equipment, and if someone lets dust fall on a fifty thousand dollar lens because they left a transom open, there is trouble.

MIKE. Your lenses got dirty.

VERONICA. Some stupid nobody, one of the useless goons who shuffle around the grounds all day — *(Beat.)* I've got to get to work. *(Blackout.)*

Scene 26

Mike waiting again. Veronica finally enters.

VERONICA. Hello.

MIKE. *I* clean the lensroom.

VERONICA. What?

MIKE. "Useless goons."

VERONICA. *What? (Beat.)* I didn't recognize you. *(Blackout.)*

Scene 27

Mike and Veronica.

MIKE. You know what we call you? We call you the vein heads.

VERONICA. Dr. Ayers said you weren't at work today.

MIKE. I took the day off.

VERONICA. That's grounds for dismissal.

MIKE. I know my job.

VERONICA. We're not vain.

MIKE. What? No, not "vain." Vein! Like you have such gigantic heads you can see the pulsating veins.

VERONICA. Did you think that up?

MIKE. No, of course not.

VERONICA. Do you know what you did?

MIKE. I didn't do a thing. I do my job correctly.

VERONICA. We have to have the lens reground.

MIKE. Look, I have to sign in and out of there just like anybody else.

VERONICA. You have ways. Sneak in and out, special keys. All your keys. You know how to get into places: that's your job.

MIKE. My *job?* What are you talking about? Look, I understand lenses.

VERONICA. No you don't.

MIKE. I understand how to —

VERONICA. *You?*

MIKE. I know their value just as well as you or Dr. Ayers.

VERONICA. It's amusing, because the whole point is that you don't stand a chance of *ever* understanding what happens when you damage precision equipment! Look at your own telescope!

MIKE. Look at you! Look at what's right in front of you! I walk around that place all day and you see me at night and you don't even know me.

VERONICA. You're usually not wearing your suit. Well how else am I supposed to know you? Up here on a hill. In the dark. Dr. Ayers — we all — rely on people like you to maintain …

MIKE. *(Scornful.)* Dr. Ayers.

VERONICA. You don't know Dr. Ayers.

MIKE. You're never there in the daytime. I am. He never leaves. He's got a sleeping bag up there.

VERONICA. He's very dedicated.

MIKE. He's very fat.

VERONICA. Brilliance and dedication. He's running calculations all day long.

MIKE. Believe me, he's not working.

VERONICA. Believe *me* —

MIKE. He's *eating.* Taking naps. He's got video games on the mainframe.

VERONICA. Listen to me. You don't get the kind of results he gets without *work.*

MIKE. He's a joke. They call him —
VERONICA. I don't care what "they" call him. You janitor. You amateur. *(Beat.)*
MIKE. Go to work.
VERONICA. Someone else will be assigned to the lensroom. *(There might be a longer blackout here than most. Stars.)*

Scene 28

Veronica and Mike address us.

VERONICA. This life does not appeal to many people.
MIKE. A lot of the best astronomy is done by people with back-yard telescopes like mine.
VERONICA. In school my friends would tell me they could not understand who would want to stay up all night and sleep all day. They said, how can you live your whole life alone, in the dark?
MIKE. The comets that hit Jupiter — they were discovered by a guy like me who just worked on the sky. I mean, he worked *every night.* I can't get out every night. When Kiki gets a movie, yes. I don't need much sleep.
VERONICA. But of course you're not living your whole life in the dark at all. Every night I see more light out there than you see in a lifetime of early mornings and lazy afternoons. It's just farther away.
MIKE. This guy's famous: him and his wife. They were a team and they were very serious. They had computer mail to other astronomers around the world and so forth. They put in a lot of time together, and that shows you what's possible with a certain amount of dedication. They're famous and they named the comet after them.
VERONICA. And you're not "alone." The myth of solitary scientific achievement is one of the most pernicious misapprehensions laymen have. I mean, Einstein at a desk in the patent office — that's their whole image. Even on the level of archetypes there's

the Curies. Why doesn't anyone ever talk about them? They worked side by side for years and won Nobels and were married and in love although he was trampled by a horse and she died of radium poisoning.

MIKE. I think about spending more time out here. "More time." Kiki would ... I mean, she gets impatient as it is. It's great for her to have her interest in film, because everybody needs to have something else to think about. For example, I come up here. I've been thinking more and more about the kind of time you need to really *see* anything. It's *serious*. You need a year just to look at the whole sky.

VERONICA. I meet all kinds of people! We all work together and there's a lot of joking and a lot of fun. There are the analysis guys, the optics guys, the guys who write the grants. I meet journalists and administrators ... custodial — uh, technicians ...

MIKE. A *year*. Light travels five trillion miles in a year. I'm going nowhere.

VERONICA. We all work together. *(Beat.)* I'm pleased to be able to tell you now officially that the probe has entered the Jupiter system proper. It has traveled four hundred million miles. *(Lights out on Veronica.)*

MIKE. I lost my job. *(Blackout. A longer one.)*

Scene 29

Mike and the telescope. We should see from Mike's clothes that it is now autumn. He has take-out cartons, papers, notebooks. Stars revolve in the sky. Fade.

Scene 30

Veronica stands facing Mike and all his junk.

VERONICA. Hello.
MIKE. Hello.
VERONICA. I haven't seen you for a while.
MIKE. No.
VERONICA. How are you doing?
MIKE. I was fired.
VERONICA. Yes, I know. I wanted to talk to you about it. *(Beat.)*
MIKE. Dr. Ayers gave me the slip. He said that you both knew that I was responsible for the lenses —
VERONICA. No!
MIKE. Even though I told you that I was not.
VERONICA. He flew into a rage. There was nothing I could do. He's very sensitive about his equipment and it's difficult for him to —
MIKE. Even though we were friends. *(Beat.)*
VERONICA. You and Dr. Ayers were friends?
MIKE. You and *me.*
VERONICA. Oh. Yes. *(Blackout.)*

Scene 31

Mike and a high pile of books and journals. He reads, checking the telescope periodically. Slow fade down. Stars spin in the sky.

Scene 32

Veronica and Mike.

VERONICA. Hello. *(Mike doesn't say anything.)* I've been travelling.

MIKE. Huh.

VERONICA. Pasadena. And then Washington. The probe is now officially orbiting Jupiter.

MIKE. I know.

VERONICA. You do? *(Mike holds up a scientific journal.)* Where did you get that?

MIKE. I *am* allowed to purchase them.

VERONICA. No, I mean. I'm just surprised.

MIKE. Surprised that I would read this.

VERONICA. Yes.

MIKE. Because you didn't think I could understand it.

VERONICA. Yes. *(Beat.)*

MIKE. Well I don't. Not much of it. I don't have the math.

VERONICA. I wouldn't think so.

MIKE. But I'm working on it. I've had a lot of time.

VERONICA. Good. *(Beat.)* If you ever want to … *discuss* … anything you've read, or are wondering about …

MIKE. Thanks.

VERONICA. Just …

MIKE. *Thanks.*

VERONICA. I didn't realize we were friends.

MIKE. Yes.

VERONICA. *(Awkward.)* I have some friends. And they're not very much like you.

MIKE. *(Dryly.)* Do go on.

VERONICA. *(Quickly.)* I see them at conferences, you know. Or at JPL this week. I always have some interesting discussions when I get back to school for a seminar …

MIKE. Or Dr. Ayers. *(Beat.)*

26

VERONICA. Yes we are friends.

MIKE. Then get me my job back.

VERONICA. We are hardly that close. I'm sorry. *(She exits. Mike watches her go. He returns to his telescope. He aims it at her. Fade.)*

Scene 33

Mike alone.

MIKE. Around the middle of *Triggerhappy* there's a scene where Esther Williams and Joel McCrea first find the natural rock amphitheater and it's at night and a big moon comes up. So their heads are silhouetted against the moon. And Esther Williams says, "Look at that moon, Shep." And Joel McCrea says "Great big beautiful moon." And Esther Williams says, "Do you think we could ever get there, Shep?" Joel McCrea: "I just don't know, honey. I reckon the moon is mighty far away." "How far away do you suppose?" "I really couldn't say, sugar." Right. Then Esther Williams says, "Farther than San Francisky?" *It is the stupidest fucking line.* Joel McCrea kind of chuckles huh huh huh. "I don't know." *You don't know?!* Yes the moon is farther away than fucking *San Francisky!* Jesus Christ, man, I mean I know you were born on the back of a horse but come on! I bought her a copy of the movie so she wouldn't have to keep renting it. Stupid stupid stupid. *(Blackout.)*

Scene 34

VERONICA. I brought you something. *(She presents a package.)* Here.

MIKE. Doctor.

VERONICA. Call me Veronica.

MIKE. Veronica.

VERONICA. Mike.

MIKE. I'm surprised.

VERONICA. Well. Don't be.

MIKE. Well. *(He opens the package. It's a Bible.)* A Bible.

VERONICA. Do you like it?

MIKE. Do I like the Bible?

VERONICA. It's all they had.

MIKE. Where did you go?

VERONICA. They uh. I got it when we went to the White House.

MIKE. *(Looking through the Bible.)* The White House?

VERONICA. There was a reception for us when the probe got to Jupiter. They've got roomfuls of them. People give them to the President, foreign leaders ... they're just lying around. I wanted to get you something nicer but I didn't have time. *(Beat.)* I feel bad.

MIKE. You stole a Bible from the White House, why should you feel bad?

VERONICA. I don't know much about gifts. I don't know what people like.

MIKE. It's okay.

VERONICA. I didn't know what you would want.

MIKE. I want my job back.

VERONICA. I have to respect Dr. Ayers' judgment. He knows what he is doing. He knows what's best for the program. He's *brilliant* ...

MIKE. He's an idiot.

VERONICA. You don't know, Mike. You just don't know. You're not there.

MIKE. I was there during the days, when you weren't there. He was in your files. In your notes.

VERONICA. My notes?

MIKE. The notebooks with your name on them. Dr. Babcock. I put them on the shelves every morning. *(Beat.)*

VERONICA. My notes. They're not *my* notes. I'm taking notes for the *team*. I — they represent common conclusions, data we've all gathered.

MIKE. *(Backing off.)* Okay.

VERONICA. They're as much Dr. Ayers' as they are mine.

MIKE. O-*kay*.

VERONICA. If anything, I'm just the medium. I *track* our observations. We're both in the *room*. I'm just writing.

MIKE. Yes.

VERONICA. Sometimes I make a few *extremely* tentative hypotheses. Tentative. Tentative.

MIKE. I understand.

VERONICA. No you don't. What do you know about methodology? You're an amateur. You don't get anything. There's nothing for you but the looking. You don't know anything, you just look.

MIKE. I look at you. *(Beat.)*

VERONICA. What do you mean? *(He lays his hand on the telescope.)* No.

MIKE. It's not very powerful. Jupiter. Mountains on the moon. And you and Dr. Ayers in the lensroom on the fourth floor on cloudy nights. They don't even let dust in there.

VERONICA. You son of a bitch.

MIKE. I need my job back.

VERONICA. No.

MIKE. You know how the lenses got damaged.

VERONICA. How dare you watch me?

MIKE. You have to track something to know what it is.

VERONICA. How dare you?

MIKE. Get me my job back.

VERONICA. I thought we were friends.

MIKE. Friends! I have *friends*. Friends are people. You know people? They have lives. They tell jokes.

VERONICA. You can't —

MIKE. You have no friends. You have colleagues and you have Dr. Ayers. Friends help each other.

VERONICA. I helped you! You never would have found Jupiter if I hadn't helped you. Not finding Jupiter is like not being able to tie your shoes.

MIKE. I know it's dark and lonely up there.

VERONICA. It is not lonely. It is not dark!

MIKE. But Dr. Ayers!

VERONICA. Dr. Ayers is the finest person I know in my field.

MIKE. I knew if I looked long enough I'd see something new.

VERONICA. You'll never see anything! You don't know me! You

29

have no job and you don't know anything! I have seen the solar system. I've seen planets. I've — *(She grabs Mike's telescope off the tripod and throws it to the ground. Beat.)*
MIKE. Get off my hill.
VERONICA. This is not your hill! *(Mike grabs her.)*
MIKE. Get off my hill! *(She struggles. He shakes her. She pulls away from him. A beat. She exits. Blackout.)*

Scene 35

VERONICA. Dr. Ayers told me he loved me on June eleventh of this year. That day the probe that we built together photographed Io, Europa, Ganymede, and Callisto and the pictures were full color and gorgeous. We were in Pasadena and we saw them develop, line by line, on the giant screens, and he held my hand. The observatory was far away, his wife was far away. It was three in the afternoon and the sun was hot and shining bright. The sun is a star that is 93 million miles away, so close it can burn you. Of course my notebooks are my own. My conclusions are tentative and occasionally speculative and they're sometimes daring and they are *private*. And of course I do most of the work. The President shook both our hands but only Dr. Ayers got photographed. When I can't stand it, I think about the pictures made by my machine floating half a billion miles away. My pictures appearing on the screen, and me standing watching in that room in California at three in the afternoon. *(Blackout.)*

Scene 36

Mike with a new telescope. He wears a heavy coat. There are more books now.

MIKE. I got a new one. It's better. It cost a lot of money but ...

The nights are good and long again. Of course it's cold. *(Lights dim. Stars. Mike goes to sleep. Blackout.)*

Scene 37

Stars. Mike is still asleep. Veronica is standing there. Mike awakes with a start.

MIKE. What? —
VERONICA. It's me. *(Beat.)*
MIKE. What is it? *(She doesn't say anything.)* What's wrong?
VERONICA. We lost the probe.
MIKE. What?
VERONICA. We lost the Jupiter probe! Did you hear me? We lost the probe!
MIKE. How?
VERONICA. It's a piece of shit.
MIKE. Come on.
VERONICA. It's a piece of shit! That's how! Did you hear me? It was a piece of shit! Dr. Ayers had been signing off on the design review checks for six years when he hadn't even been looking at them so consequently he failed to notice that the probe was a piece of shit!
MIKE. Jesus. I'm sorry. Do you know what happened?
VERONICA. It got to the Jovian system and it. Oh God.
MIKE. Veronica. What happened? What happened?
VERONICA. It bumped into it.
MIKE. Bumped into Jupiter?
VERONICA. Yes.
MIKE. How can it "bump into" Jupiter?
VERONICA. What do you mean how can it bump into it?! Jupiter is not only the largest but also the most massive fucking planet in the solar system!
MIKE. Okay! Okay!
VERONICA. I thought you knew that!

31

MIKE. I did, you're right.

VERONICA. Jesus.

MIKE. You're right.

VERONICA. It was supposed to be a close approach, but Dr. Ayers — oh God. *(Beat.)* Jesus God it's cold up here. I'm sorry to wake you.

MIKE. It's okay. I'm sorry.

VERONICA. Yes. *(Beat.)* I just thought you'd like to know. *(Blackout.)*

Scene 38

Same setup.

VERONICA. Mike?

MIKE. What?

VERONICA. You look frozen. I have coffee.

MIKE. I'm okay.

VERONICA. I've got a thermos, here. Take this. Drink it. *(She pours.)*

MIKE. All right.

VERONICA. It's very clear tonight.

MIKE. Why do you think I'm up here?

VERONICA. I know.

MIKE. This is hot.

VERONICA. Sip it. *(Beat.)* Do you want some vodka?

MIKE. Yeah?

VERONICA. Yes. Do you want some in your coffee?

MIKE. Sure. *(She pours. Beat.)*

VERONICA. They fired me too.

MIKE. What?

VERONICA. Dr. Ayers.

MIKE. Veronica.

VERONICA. They needed somebody to blame, you know, for the probe. And my name was all over the project.

MIKE. But it wasn't your fault. You can prove it.

VERONICA. No. They took everything. All my work, sealed off. I can't even get my notebooks back.

MIKE. I can't believe it.

VERONICA. I know. Neither can I. It's cold. *(Beat as they drink.)* Orion, winter constellation, you know it?

MIKE. "The hunter."

VERONICA. Right. See the stars in the belt? One of them is Betelgeuse, the red giant. It was my favorite star when I was a kid. And one of them, look to the left, can you see it?

MIKE. I think so.

VERONICA. It's a binary. A binary system. Two stars —

MIKE. Two stars in orbit around each other.

VERONICA. Good. Most people can't see both. They're too close together and one is very faint. Americans Indians had a test for vision. If you could pick out the binary in Orion, if you could see both stars then your vision was perfect and you could be a hunter. It's just a coincidence, hunter, hunter. Two completely different cultures and everything. *(Beat.)* Can you see both?

MIKE. Yes.

VERONICA. Yes. So can I. *(Blackout.)*

Scene 39

Mike is asleep. Veronica enters.

VERONICA. *(Softly.)* Mike. Mike. *(Mike stirs.)* Mike. What are you doing up here?

MIKE. Observing. I'm waiting for the planets.

VERONICA. Mike, it's cold. It's supposed to get down to freezing tonight.

MIKE. I know. That's called "winter." *(Blackout.)*

Scene 40

Mike lying down. Veronica has a heavy blanket. She holds it out.

VERONICA. Your coat doesn't look very warm.
MIKE. I'm okay.
VERONICA. Here. *(She puts the blanket on him.)* Maybe you should go home.
MIKE. I'm okay.
VERONICA. Go home, Mike. I'll help you. Come on.
MIKE. No. It's okay.
VERONICA. Come on. *(She tries to help. He pushes her away.)* They're predicting single digits. I want to help.
MIKE. I don't need help. *(Blackout.)*

Scene 41

Mike asleep. Veronica sitting under the blanket.

VERONICA. Mike.
MIKE. Uh?
VERONICA. Wake up.
MIKE. What?
VERONICA. I know about Kiki.
MIKE. What?
VERONICA. She's gone, right? *(Beat.)* You haven't been together in a while. Months, I think.
MIKE. She's away on a trip.
VERONICA. I'm very sorry.
MIKE. A little vacation. She likes to watch movies at night. I

34

come up here.

VERONICA. Mike.

MIKE. Good night.

VERONICA. She packed everything. She wasn't going on a trip.

MIKE. How do you know?

VERONICA. Oh for God's sake, Mike. We had a forty-seven inch mirror on the hill. I can count eyelashes.

MIKE. You were spying?

VERONICA. Did you think we watched Jupiter all night long? No. I'm not proud of it. It was something Dr. Ayers enjoyed.

MIKE. How can you do that?

VERONICA. Is that a technical question or ethical?

MIKE. Technical.

VERONICA. Please, Mike. I thought you understood the kind of power we have. That mirror was polished in a cave in Kentucky for nine years. Has someone in town been drinking? We knew because we can see swollen capillaries in an eyeball five miles away.

MIKE. She packed everything. She had ten boxes.

VERONICA. Sixteen. She shipped six UPS a few nights before she left.

MIKE. How many nights were you watching me?

VERONICA. A few. I was worried. *(Mike gets up and looks through the telescope.)*

MIKE. There's the room. There's the depression she made in the couch. She said I was never home and that she didn't love me. And that I was an unemployed janitor and that I didn't love her either. She said that I hadn't even *thought* about her, she was pretty sure, for about a year. *(Looks up at the sky.)* Yep. It'll be a year in a month. *(Fade.)*

Scene 42

Veronica. Mike's junk is still there but no Mike. She looks around, worried. Beat. Mike enters, in his jumpsuit.

MIKE. Hello.
VERONICA. Mike. Are you okay? Where —
MIKE. Here. *(Hands her a package.)*
VERONICA. *(Confused.)* Thanks … *(She opens it.)* My notebooks.
MIKE. I didn't know what you would like.
VERONICA. How did you — ?
MIKE. I know how to get into places. You were right. *(Jangles keys.)* My keys. In this case, duplicates of my keys that I made right after Dr. Ayers canned me.
VERONICA. Mike. Do you know what's in these? Do you?
MIKE. Yes. *(Blackout.)*

Scene 43

Veronica. The hill has been cleared of all the junk. Mike enters, dressed for warmer weather. He carries his telescope and a pile of books.

MIKE. Well hello.
VERONICA. Hello.
MIKE. How's work?
VERONICA. I want to thank you.
MIKE. Don't.
VERONICA. I thought I wouldn't be working for a long time, Mike. You were the only one who could have helped.

MIKE. You did the work. I remembered what you had been working on. I've done enough on my own to know how much you did, and what was in your books. And I knew something about Dr. Ayers' work habits.

VERONICA. You impressed the investigating commission.

MIKE. Well ... that wasn't what it was about.

VERONICA. No.

MIKE. How is Dr. Ayers?

VERONICA. I guess he's pretty comfortable. It's minimum security, so he can play tennis, you know, get outside.

MIKE. Oh, good.

VERONICA. We really don't communicate any more.

MIKE. Good. *(Beat.)* Hey, listen. I owe you too ... a month ago, you know. The coffee and the blanket. The vodka and and everything. It was nice of you.

VERONICA. *(Embarrassed.)* It's okay. I was glad.

MIKE. Thanks. *(Beat.)*

VERONICA. Are you working?

MIKE. Yeah. Different cleaning gig, you know, but it's good.

VERONICA. Good.

MIKE. So. *(Mike looks excited.)*

VERONICA. So.

MIKE. So this research that you're doing. I'm wondering ...

VERONICA. Yes?

MIKE. I'd like to ask about it because I've been working on something. From some things you said and some things I've been working on on my own. Here. *(He unpacks his books.)* I want to show you something. This happened months ago. Almost a year ago. I noticed an object. And I've been tracking it.

VERONICA. You have?

MIKE. Yes! And here, see I took observations every night, after I got serious, you know, and I kept notes, here they are ...

VERONICA. Mike!

MIKE. I know. I plotted the motion. I tracked it. Charts ... And I think I'm working toward something new, you know. Something original. Remember I asked you about how —

VERONICA. Yes, yes!

MIKE. So I've been meaning to ask you about it. Consult. I was

37

going to look you up but now here you are.

VERONICA. Yes.

MIKE. Veronica, take a look at this. I don't know what to make of it. I'm pretty excited, I admit.

VERONICA. Well, let me take a look at it. Mike, you did a beautiful job with these observations. This looks professional.

MIKE. Thanks. There were some nights when I couldn't get an accurate reading, you know, for whatever reason. But that's par for the course, like you said, there are cloudy nights, you learn that.

VERONICA. Uh huh. Now you've got …

MIKE. It's continued here.

VERONICA. Right. *(Beat.)*

MIKE. So.

VERONICA. Oh.

MIKE. Uh huh?

VERONICA. Oh God.

MIKE. So? What have I got?

VERONICA. Mike.

MIKE. What? Tell me.

VERONICA. Mike, this is Comet 69P/Taylor.

MIKE. What?

VERONICA. 69P/Taylor. Visible from Earth every seventeen years. Discovered 1915.

MIKE. 69P/Taylor? — Are you sure?

VERONICA. Yes. It's an old favorite. I'm sorry. *(Beat.)*

MIKE. Shit.

VERONICA. These are beautiful observations.

MIKE. I'm an idiot. I'm an idiot!

VERONICA. Mike, you're not. These observations are textbook. They're graduate level and you did it by yourself. With your telescope. They're just not new. And that's fine. Something new only happens once in a great while. This is important work. You have to track something to know what it is. Now you really know what it is.

MIKE. I worked on that for a *year.*

VERONICA. It's okay. You'll work on something new this year. It's a whole new year. *(Beat.)* I'll help you. We can do something together.

MIKE. No. That's all right. Thanks. I —

VERONICA. Mike. I want to. *(Mike nods. Blackout.)*

Scene 44

Veronica addresses us.

VERONICA. Giovanni Schiaparelli. I like that name. He was an Italian astronomer. He was the first to notice the valleys and canyons carved into the surface of Mars. In 1877 he sent the news of his discovery all around the world: "Canali." Channels. But when the news got to America someone forgot to translate from the Italian and everyone thought that *canals* had been discovered on the surface of the red planet. Canals? Water; irrigation; farming: Civilization. Cities made of glass. You can see how the argument went. People got excited. And my predecessors in this profession spent years beating their heads against the wall trying to correct the impression. There are no *canals* on Mars. And no Martians. There's not even any water, for God's sake. Well. Now. In my lifetime we have sent spacecraft to Mars. And there is beginning to be some good evidence to suggest that many millions of years ago there was water there. Now there is no life on Mars and there probably never was. But there were oceans and ice and rivers. So who knows? You'll have to forgive me for going on in a speculative vein. But it is important to maintain enough flexibility to revise an opinion, and then to revise the revision. We are learning all the time. And it takes a while to figure some things out. *(Fade. Stars.)*

Curtain

MISS YOU

MISS YOU was first produced at the HBO Comedy Arts Festival in Aspen, Colorado, on January 5, 1997. It was directed by James Eckhouse. The cast was as follows:

WOMAN 1, 2 .... Lisa Edelstein
MAN 1, 2 .... Jerry Levine

Four characters: Man, Woman, Man 2, Woman 2, to be played by two actors.

MISS YOU

Man and Woman on the phone.

WOMAN. Hello?
MAN. I miss you!
WOMAN. Oh, hi.
MAN. Miss me?
WOMAN. Uh huh.
MAN. Really?
WOMAN. Yes. Yes I do: I miss you.
MAN. A lot?
WOMAN. Yes.
MAN. How much?
WOMAN. I told you, a lot.
MAN. God, I miss you.
WOMAN. Mm.
MAN. I wish you were here.
WOMAN. Yes.
MAN. I wish you were here right now.
WOMAN. Mm.
MAN. I wish I was *there.*
WOMAN. Uh huh.
MAN. I wish I could be there with you: I mean I really *miss* you.
I have a —
WOMAN. I know.
MAN. I have a —
WOMAN. Can you hold on?
MAN. I have a little sur —
WOMAN. Can you hold on a sec? I've got another call.
MAN. S (ure) — *(Beat. She clicks over.)*
WOMAN. Hello?
MAN 2. Hey.

43

WOMAN. Oh, God. Oh God hi! Oh hi! God, hi!

MAN 2. Hey.

WOMAN. Hi, God, you called! I was hoping you'd — where have you been? Hi! Thank you for calling! How are you?

MAN 2. I'm fine.

WOMAN. Great.

MAN 2. How are —

WOMAN. Great. Wonderful. Now! *Hi.* When can I see you? Are you free? Are you busy? I can get time. Do you want to get something to eat tonight? Or we can cook. I can shop and we can — We can stay in. *We can cook here,* I've got wine. *Come over.* Come over now if you want. I miss you.

MAN 2. Listen —

WOMAN. I miss you. Yesterday afternoon was — the museum was wonderful (I can't believe I live right here in the city and I *never* go), and the walk, and the river. And the ice cream! Unh! *Nothing* has ever tasted so good to me in my life, I swear to God, it was — and drinks by the — and dinner, and *God* you looked so — and last night was —

MAN 2. Listen, there's some things I should do but we ought to try to get together.

WOMAN. Try? Try to get together? Yes, I think we should "try"! I mean, yes. *Yes.* That would be great. Tonight? Do you want to set something up for tonight? *(Beat.)*

MAN 2. Tonight?

WOMAN. Yes. We could —

MAN 2. Look, can I call you back?

WOMAN. What?

MAN 2. I gotta call you back.

WOMAN. Okay, but call me right —

MAN 2. Yeah. I'll call you. I'll talk to you. Okay?

WOMAN. Soon. I'll talk to you, okay —

MAN 2. Bye. *(Beat.)*

WOMAN. Bye — *(She almost hangs up.)* Shit — *(Clicks over.)* Hello?

MAN. Hello?

WOMAN. It's me.

MAN. *I missed you!*

WOMAN. I'm sorry. I couldn't get —

MAN. I'm coming home.

WOMAN. What?

MAN. I'm calling because I'm coming home. It's my surprise. I'm cutting things short. I'm at the airport!

WOMAN. Why?

MAN. I'm about to get on an airplane.

WOMAN. No, why — you're cutting things short? Can you do that?

MAN. Yes. I worked straight through. I haven't slept for two days so I'd get done early because I *missed* you and I'm —

WOMAN. Wait. Hold —

MAN. We take off in ten minutes. They're pre-boarding now. I'm carrying my — I want to give you my arrival time so you can come get me. I've only got carry-on so don't come to the gate, don't park, just pull up at arriving flights and I'll be —

WOMAN. 'Nother call, sorry, I —

MAN. Honey, wait, I'm about to board, I don't want to miss my —

WOMAN. *(Clicks over.)* Hello?

MAN. No, it's still me. Don't go I don't want to miss my —

WOMAN. Sorry, *hold on. (Clicks.) Hello? Hello?*

MAN 2. Hey, me.

WOMAN. Oh *hi!*

MAN 2. Hey. Listen. I —

WOMAN. That was *fast!* You're —

MAN 2. Listen, I just realized, I've got a lot of things to take care of.

WOMAN. Uh huh.

MAN 2. So I think we better —

WOMAN. What?

MAN 2. I think we better take a rain check on tonight.

WOMAN. A rain check.

MAN 2. We'll do it some other time.

WOMAN. You have a lot of *things* to take care of?

MAN 2. Yeah.

WOMAN. What things?

MAN 2. I should get some sleep. I have to get up early.

WOMAN. We spend the day together yesterday. You didn't have things to take care of. Yesterday turned into last night and it was a long sleepless night and that seemed fine with you then; it seemed wonderful to me —

MAN 2. We'll have to do it another time.

WOMAN. I don't have another *time*. This is the *time*. Do you see? Let's do this *now*. I'm sorry. I just mean, while we can. We shouldn't miss this. Yesterday came out of nowhere. We were together. It was *great*. I loved it. I loved being with you. I loved you. *(Beat.)* Did you hear me? I love you. Can you hear me? Are you there?

MAN 2. Can you hold on a minute?

WOMAN. What?

MAN 2. I've got another call coming in.

WOMAN. Don't take it!

MAN 2. I have to —

WOMAN. They'll call back.

MAN 2. I'll just be —

WOMAN. *Don't* — *(He clicks over.)*

MAN 2. Hello? *(Beat.)*

WOMAN 2. Do you think I'm stupid?

MAN 2. Hello?

WOMAN 2. *You fucking asshole.*

MAN 2. Honey?

WOMAN 2. Do you think I'm *stupid?* Do you think I'm just sort of unaware of what's going on around me? I'm not *stupid,* you fucking jerk. You're the fucking idiot loser —

MAN 2. Honey, what are you —

WOMAN 2. "Honey"? I saw you at the *museum.* *"Honey."* Little stroll by the *river?* I saw you buying little mmmmmm, oooooh! ice kweem cones, so cute! Mm, mine's really good, here have a taste, no go ahead, it's so good, here, you've got to have one, mmmm — You bastard! How could you do this? You take her to *our restaurant, "honey"?* (I followed you. I'm not stupid.) You get home from the "office" at *four-thirty in the morning?* Well, listen up: Fuck you, and fuck the art museum and your little ice cream scoopy friend, and fuck you again, because I wash my hands of you and good riddance, you're gonna rot in hell you lying sleazebag dumbshit fuckball. *(She hangs up. Beat. Man 2 clicks back.)*

MAN 2. Hello?

WOMAN. Hello? *(Beat.)*

MAN 2. You still want to get together?

WOMAN. Tonight?

MAN 2. Sure. We could get something to eat.

WOMAN. You changed your mind.

MAN 2. Yeah.

WOMAN. What about your things?

MAN 2. What?

WOMAN. The things you have to do.

MAN 2. They can wait.

WOMAN. You have to sleep.

MAN 2. I'll sleep at your place.

WOMAN. You will. *(Beat.)* I'm sorry.

MAN 2. What?

WOMAN. I have to go.

MAN 2 What? Why?

WOMAN. I'll have to call you back. I have another call. I just remembered.

MAN 2. Listen, let's just —

WOMAN. He called me first. I have to go. Okay? He —

MAN 2. Come on, forget about —

WOMAN. I should talk to him. I think he's very tired. He hasn't slept. He went without sleep for two days. *(Beat.)*

MAN 2. Wai — *(Beat. She clicks over.)*

WOMAN. Hi. It's me. Hello? Hello? Are you there? *(Beat.)*

MAN. I missed my flight.

WOMAN. I'm sorry.

MAN. It just took off.

WOMAN. I'm sorry. Is there another one tonight?

MAN. I don't know. I'll check. Probably. Probably late.

WOMAN. Take it. I'll pick you up.

MAN. You will?

WOMAN. Tell me when.

MAN. It'll be late.

WOMAN. I don't care how late. I'll come to the gate.

MAN. You will?

WOMAN. Yes.

MAN. Don't miss me.

WOMAN. I won't.

Curtain

DAMAGE CONTROL

DAMAGE CONTROL was first produced at the One Dream Theater in New York City on August 12, 1994. It was directed by David Auburn. The cast was as follows:

AVERY .... Steve Mitchell
DAVENPORT .... Mark Gerrard

DAMAGE CONTROL

A bedroom. Avery and Davenport look into a mirror, i.e., at us. They wear business suits. Avery is a middle-aged man. Davenport is younger.

AVERY. How do I look?

DAVENPORT. Fine.

AVERY. Fine?

DAVENPORT. You look very good. You're set.

AVERY. Look at this, I'm a grown man.

DAVENPORT. Yes?

AVERY. And I have to ask another grown man how I look. That's where I am. Is the tie all right?

DAVENPORT. It's fine.

AVERY. Fine?

DAVENPORT. It's really fine.

AVERY. The knot?

DAVENPORT. Wonderful. So we are set. Is there anything you'd like to go over?

AVERY. Can you imagine? I picked it out myself. I select my own tie from an assortment of ties that I keep in my own closet in my *bedroom*, and this becomes a source of anxiety for me, because I picked it out.

DAVENPORT. It looks wonderful. Let's talk setting, sir.

AVERY. You have "experts" coming to you with assortments. Approved ties, an "approved selection" by a "color expert." It becomes a battle to pick a tie by yourself. I say to myself, am I twelve years old?

DAVENPORT. Ha. Would you like to review your marks before we go downstairs, sir?

AVERY. You spend a lifetime bickering with your wife about, "hurry up, we're late, you look fine ... *we're late*" — and now she's

51

blowing past you while you loiter in the closet like a sissy. Oh! Oh! Blue? Red? Paisleys? Little chevrons? Stripes —

DAVENPORT. No paisleys!

AVERY. I know! I like paisley. God forbid I should wear I tie I like.

DAVENPORT. It reads "fussy."

AVERY. You're wearing a paisley tie.

DAVENPORT. Well, I'm not going to be on TV.

AVERY. And, you're fussy! So, I'm set with the school tie. Blue stripe, gold stripe, red stripe. Stripey, stripey, stripey, stripey.

DAVENPORT. Sir, I can see you — I'm just going to give you a minute.

AVERY. Good. *(Beat.)* A lot of the guys, most of the guys aren't even picking out their own suits, they get some little fop who comes in from God knows where ...

DAVENPORT. I'll wait downstairs.

AVERY. Yes.

DAVENPORT. You'll be okay for a few seconds?

AVERY. Yes. Hello? Yes!

DAVENPORT. Okay, great. *(Davenport starts to exit.)*

AVERY. Where's my handkerchief?

DAVENPORT. Oh ...

AVERY. Jesus God, did I leave it ...

DAVENPORT. I thought we decided, sir.

AVERY. What?

DAVENPORT. I thought we agreed, no handkerchief.

AVERY. When?

DAVENPORT. There was a memo.

AVERY. I didn't see it.

DAVENPORT. We agreed it was too "fussy."

AVERY. What if I have to blow my nose?

DAVENPORT. Most people don't use a handkerchief. The average person ... it's in the memo. It's a visual thing, it tends not to play ...

AVERY. Give me something. I could sneeze, you know. Jesus, I always have a hanky. Where's the memo? I always have a hanky.

DAVENPORT. Well now there are two ways to go on this. It's a TV thing. You don't ... well, A., you don't want to be blowing your nose on TV, anyway, right? *(Laughs.)*

AVERY. *(Irritable.)* I know that.

DAVENPORT. Right …

AVERY. For God's sake.

DAVENPORT. But if, worst-case, you did, you don't want to pull the white hanky out because the handkerchief denotes a whole patrician world of privilege and so forth, chauffeurs, Andover, custom tailoring … the *monogrammed handkerchief* … it's fussy …

AVERY. I have a goddamned head cold! What am I, not supposed to get sick? Give me some Kleenex or something.

DAVENPORT. Ooh. Uh, polling says that's not the way to go: it reads sloppy, potentially unprepared.

AVERY. Give me one now. I'm going to sneeze.

DAVENPORT. Oh. We don't have uh …

AVERY. Give me a paper towel!

DAVENPORT. Oh … *(Avery has a sneezing fit. Over it:)* But, just as a note, you just want to back-back burner, uh, keep in mind Kleenex is a registered trademark, not a generic term, though it has come to be used as one … so you want to say "facial tissue" if it comes up — not that it will, that would be — just like you want to avoid "Xerox" — registered TM — so go with "photocopy," or "photocopier" if you're referring to a device for making copies … *(Avery's fit ends. He gasps for breath.)*

AVERY. Uh. Uh.

DAVENPORT. Good, now let me just … *(Davenport grabs the back of Avery's jacket and pulls it down sharply, then smoothes the collar around Avery's neck.)*

AVERY. *(Loosens his tie, breathes sharply.)* Get away from me!

DAVENPORT. It was riding up, sir!

AVERY. *(Ripping off his tie.)* Just take a step back.

DAVENPORT. Sir, your tie!

AVERY. Give me some air! I need some air. Can you let me breathe for thirty seconds at a time?

DAVENPORT. I'm sorry, I …

AVERY. Just take a step back! I'll do the tie. I'll do it. I know how to do it. I've known how to tie a tie for almost fifty years! I can do it now, for God's sake! *(Beat.)*

DAVENPORT. Yes sir. I'm sorry if I suggested …

AVERY. It's all right.

DAVENPORT. I'm just trying provide another perspective if and when. Feedback. I'm support, that's all, I'm here for when …

AVERY. My wife gives me feedback, Davenport.

DAVENPORT. Right. I'm sorry.

AVERY. A woman who knows how to dress. She doesn't pick out my ties but she consults. Now I spend more time getting dressed in the morning than she does! That's what's happening to all of us: we're turning into a bunch of mannequins. You know those male models, Davenport? *(Avery strikes an Arrow shirt ad pose.)*

DAVENPORT. Ha ha. *(Joking.)* Don't use that downstairs!

AVERY. I won't, you idiot.

DAVENPORT. Oh, I was just …

AVERY. Jesus. This tie. I hate this tie. Give me another one.

DAVENPORT. Look, sir, I was just. Look, I've been wanting to review the whole program.

AVERY. Give me that green stripe. *(Davenport fetches the tie. Avery puts it on.)*

DAVENPORT. I'd feel a lot better — I don't know about you but *I'd* feel a lot better if you could let me just run through it. Okay? Now everything is set up right in front of the house.

AVERY. Why does it have to be my own house for God's sake?

DAVENPORT. Sir, there was a memo. It's …

AVERY. My own house!

DAVENPORT. It's a trust thing, sir, and your house has been a major asset in the past. During the campaign? Remember? The shrubbery speech?

AVERY. It was a good speech.

DAVENPORT. The people like your house, sir. It's familiar. So. You come out and the set-ups have you right out in front.

AVERY. In front of the shrub again?

DAVENPORT. Yes sir. The shrub will be in shot.

AVERY. Good.

DAVENPORT. We made sure of that.

AVERY. We just had them trimmed. My wife did.

DAVENPORT. I know. That will be extra-good. Everything will be fine. And then afterwards, what, sir?

AVERY. I used to go out there myself. Saturday afternoon, with the shears. Summer afternoon …

DAVENPORT. Sir?

AVERY. Drinking iced tea. Southern women know how to make iced tea. They call it "sweet tea." Cool as a kiss.

DAVENPORT. Afterwards, *what*, sir?

AVERY. Afterwards, it's over. What are you talking about?

DAVENPORT. No questions!

AVERY. Oh for Godsake do you think I want to answer any questions?

DAVENPORT. No.

AVERY. Jesus. You are ... why don't you go downstairs?

DAVENPORT. I wanted to go over everything.

AVERY. Well, I know it! All right?

DAVENPORT. I know you know it. It's a ... heh, it's really about my comfort level more than anything else.

AVERY. Well who gives a shit about your comfort level? *(Davenport doesn't know what to say.)* Well?

DAVENPORT. Well this is an important ...

AVERY. I know it's important! Agh! This tie! Where are my ties? Get me another tie!

DAVENPORT. Yes sir. I ... I've worked very hard on this. Not that that's a measure of its importance, that's not what I'm ... well, we've all worked hard on this. We think there's a very very good possibility that it could go beautifully, and ...

AVERY. No, not that tie! Who taught you about ties, Davenport?

DAVENPORT. Sir?

AVERY. Your Daddy? My Daddy taught me.

DAVENPORT. Ha. That's wonderful sir.

AVERY. Well who taught you?

DAVENPORT. I really don't remember. But that's great.

AVERY. What's great?

DAVENPORT. That image. It's a really great image, a great father-son thing.

AVERY. Where'd you learn to tie your necktie, Davenport?

DAVENPORT. Oh I just picked it up.

AVERY. Your Daddy didn't teach you?

DAVENPORT. No.

AVERY. You're sure?

DAVENPORT. Yes. My father died when I was quite young, sir. I never really knew him.

AVERY. Oh. I'm sorry.

DAVENPORT. No, it's all right. I never knew him.

AVERY. *(Impatient.)* Yes, I'm sorry you never knew him.

DAVENPORT. Oh. Thank you. But that's all right.

AVERY. Well. Ha. Well, those are the breaks.

DAVENPORT. Yes.

AVERY. As my wife says, you roll with the punches.

DAVENPORT. Yes!

AVERY. Legs.

DAVENPORT. *(Confused.)* Yes.

AVERY. Legs!

DAVENPORT. Oh. I ... what?

AVERY. The legs on the woman. I swear to God she made a pact with Satan. Her stride. She covers about a yard at a time, wouldn't you say so?

DAVENPORT. Oh yes. I think we're about ready sir.

AVERY. ... At least. Purposeful. A very purposeful woman. Very beautiful woman. *(Beat.)* Loosen your necktie, Davenport.

DAVENPORT. Sir?

AVERY. Undo it.

DAVENPORT. Sir, there are some time factors here, and we're coming down to it.

AVERY. Undo your tie, Davenport.

DAVENPORT. Sir, I'm dressed sir.

AVERY. Goddamn it. *(He starts at Davenport. Davenport jumps back, then loosens his tie.)* There. You have a goddamn prissy knot in your tie.

DAVENPORT. I ...

AVERY. *That* reads "fussy." You think you're the only one who thinks about these things? How do you think I got where I am? I didn't always have little furry creatures like you sniffing around my armpits every moment. I was on my own for a long time. Come here.

DAVENPORT. Sir ... *(He pulls Davenport in front of him and wraps his arms around Davenport's chest. He starts tying his tie.)*

AVERY. In the time-honored tradition. My father (and no doubt your father too would have if he hadn't ... you know) took me in front of the mirror like this. Of course I was much shorter pro-portionally than you are. Did you know every twentieth-century president has been over six feet tall? And Churchill. Half Windsor … a good knot, the only one I use. Who taught you yours? You don't know, I know: a prissy knot. Watch my hands. Over the top … and back under … and up and through … and pull it tight and it should be a very tight triangular knot. Do you see that?

DAVENPORT. Yes sir. Time is …

AVERY. *(Rips open the tie again.)* Now you try it.

DAVENPORT. Now?

AVERY. Do it. This is a knot a woman likes to tighten. *(Davenport tries the knot.)* I think of my wife's fingers straightening my tie. Before a fundraiser. Before a public appearance. Thousands of dinners, thousands of pieces of chicken. My wife has very long fingers, Davenport. Very knowing fingers. No, not like that, you idiot, you've messed it up. Undo it and do it again! Undo it! Putting in time. We called it "the wilderness." Handshakes, speeches, handshakes. The same speeches, the same jokes. Notecards with names and professions written on them. My wife kept a file. At one point we had almost three thousand names. She would quiz me on planes, in the van on the way to and from the airport. "Dick Ehrenkranz?" "General contracting, Meade County Chamber of Commerce, Georgia Tech, Elks, wife Marybeth, daughter Whitney, son Chris, tennis." Bam bam bam. I could rattle them off. My wife kept all the cards. Nothing escaped her. Whenever I turned around, she was there, with her cards and her smile, and her elegant gowns and her yellow hair. That hair was bright yellow, Davenport.

DAVENPORT. I've seen pictures.

AVERY. I mean you had to shield your eyes when she was standing in a bright light. You're not interested in that, Davenport. You care about handkerchiefs clashing with my cufflinks on TV. There, that's right. Doesn't that look better?

DAVENPORT. It's too tight.

AVERY. It will always be too tight. Part of being a man is learning how to live with that pain. *(Beat.)* I've been thinking, Davenport. I've been thinking I shouldn't say "deeply regret."

DAVENPORT. It's all programmed in, sir. We worked it all out.

AVERY. What about "profoundly"?

DAVENPORT. "Profoundly regret"?

AVERY. Yes.

DAVENPORT. I don't know, the press will take it as an ad lib because we're distributing copies of the statements, so it could read sincerity but it could also read glib. "Profoundly regret." "Profoundly regret ... "

AVERY. Well I don't want to say "deeply regret" and "apologize deeply."

DAVENPORT. You don't say both.

AVERY. Yes I do, Davenport, I was going over it.

DAVENPORT. Okay, say, "apologize profoundly." *(To himself.)* "Apologize profoundly, apologize profoundly ... "

AVERY. You should wear a narrower tie with your build.

DAVENPORT. I take it back.

AVERY. Let me get you a tie.

DAVENPORT. The tie is fine, sir. Look, I think you should just stick to the text as written. It's too confusing otherwise, and ...

AVERY. Take off the paisley. I don't like it.

DAVENPORT. I ...

AVERY. If I can't wear it you can't wear it. You're a little guy, so no stripes either. I've got little green anchors!

DAVENPORT. No. We don't — did you hear what I said? "Deeply regret" *and* "Apologize deeply."

AVERY. Little green anchors! Here you go Davenport.

DAVENPORT. No! We don't have time.

AVERY. Come here! *(He grabs Davenport again. Davenport struggles.)*

DAVENPORT. No sir!

AVERY. Little green anchors!

DAVENPORT. Sir, we don't ... Let go!

AVERY. Come here, Davenport. *(Avery wrestles with Davenport. Davenport wiggles out of his grip. Avery gets a hold of Davenport's tie and pulls. Davenport chokes. He is strangling.)*

DAVENPORT. Goddamn it! *(Avery rips off Davenport's tie. Davenport doubles over, gasping for breath.)*

AVERY. *(Holding up the tie.)* There. Isn't that better?

DAVENPORT. I quit!

AVERY. Stop whining.

DAVENPORT. You have to go now! You're going to ruin everything!

AVERY. *(Starts to fasten the new tie on Davenport.)* I don't think
... here's where I think we need a change: I don't think I should
say "minor."

DAVENPORT. Let me go.

AVERY. No. *(Beat.)* I don't think I should say "minor."

DAVENPORT. It's the legal term.

AVERY. What about "juvenile."

DAVENPORT. God no, are you out of your mind?

AVERY. "Adolescent."

DAVENPORT. No.

AVERY. "Pre-pubescent."

DAVENPORT. You're making me sick!

AVERY. Well what? You're feedback, give me feedback!

DAVENPORT. How about "adolescent vixen?" That's what you
want to say.

AVERY. Knock it off, Davenport.

DAVENPORT. How about "Statutory rapee"? No: "Temptress"!
That always plays well in the press. How about "Pre-teen
Temptress"? Save them some work, write the headline.

AVERY. So, stick with "minor"? It sounds so legal.

DAVENPORT. I didn't want "minor"! I wanted the generic "mistakes were made" acknowledgement! I wanted "I am flawed! But
this regrettable and profound error in judgement in no way
impedes my ability to carry out the duties and responsibilities of
my office or to complete my appointed term!"

AVERY. That's good. Are we using that?

DAVENPORT. No!

AVERY. Why not?

DAVENPORT. It's not enough! Everybody knows that! I am
quitting. As soon as this is over I am quitting.

AVERY. That's too much.

DAVENPORT. No, *I* am quitting! Now we are not going to keep
them waiting —

AVERY. "I am flawed." I liked that. "I am flawed."

DAVENPORT. We don't have time for this! You stupid stupid old
— you've already ruined everything! You can't ruin this! My career.
I thought I had backed a sure thing. I thought, Communications
Director ... I'm quitting. I've got to get resumes out. They'll

59

laugh. But who could have handled this? Show me the guy who could have handled this. I *tried*. We all tried. You are saying "I have disgraced my family and forever sullied the dignity of this high office" and that's it!

AVERY. Did you write that, Davenport?

DAVENPORT. I was on the drafting committee.

AVERY. With my wife.

DAVENPORT. Yes.

AVERY. Yes. She keeps her hand in.

DAVENPORT. She keeps the focus. *(Beat.)*

AVERY. Which part was hers? "Forever sullied the dignity of my office"?

DAVENPORT. No.

AVERY. The other thing.

DAVENPORT. Yes. *(Beat.)*

AVERY. I liked "I am flawed."

DAVENPORT. You can't say it. She won't let you. She hates you. Do you know that? She hates you. She kept us in there drafting that thing for days. She loved it. Are you ready?

AVERY. "I have disgraced my family … " My family. My Daddy? My mother. My wife. My father showed me how to tie a tie. My children.

DAVENPORT. Where's the paisley?

AVERY. "And forever sullied the dignity of this high office." *(Beat.)* Well. How do I look?

DAVENPORT. Fine. Wonderful.

AVERY. Well. All right. *(Beat.)* There's no sense putting it off.

Blackout

60

THREE MONOLOGUES

THREE MONOLOGUES was first performed at the Middlebury College Department of Theater in Middlebury, Vermont, on November 23, 1998. It was directed by Carl Forsman. The cast was as follows:

WOMAN .... Courtney Brocks

THREE MONOLOGUES

1.

I'm alone, and it's good. I have a book. I took off the paper cover and I like the feel of the cloth on my hands. Thick pages and a thick book and the pages aren't trimmed perfect so you can run your fingers along the spine and along the other side — the edges of the pages — and it's very tactile. I've got all day. It's quiet. When it's quiet I can read twenty-five pages an hour. It's a 600-page book so a couple of good quiet days and I can put it away. The story is very interesting and you want to know what happens next. But it's not just a potboiler. There are descriptions — of landscapes, costumes, someone's voice, what a ship looks like — that are very well-written. Twenty-five pages an hour.

But sometimes I'm reading along and I look up and I don't remember anything that's happened. I've been turning the pages, my eyes have been faithfully scanning the lines, but I'm lost. Maybe just a couple of words have stuck, leftover: NICETY. FULL-LIPPED. AGHAST. So I have to go back. And the paragraphs — the ones that don't advance the plot, but are descriptive. Some have been assembled so carefully, with such a researcher's eye for detail and physician's sense of anatomy, that I get caught. My eyes get trapped inside the cracks and folds of sentences and in the spaces after punctuation where the sentences are joined — I lose time there too.

So twenty-five pages and an hour, or two, or an afternoon, go by. And it gets dark. And my legs are folded under me and they cramp and fall asleep and it is a terrible, painful effort to get up to pour myself the glass of water I feel I will die if I don't drink.

2.

Today we're together. You're wearing a parka, it's red.

(It's the kind worn by skiers. Not modern skiers with helmets and Batman suits and sliding down mountains like mercury. You're a skiier from 1930. You have wooden skis and bamboo ski poles. You're an Alpine skier-hiker. You're on an Excursion. You've got a leather rucksack and a cloth cap with ear flaps. You have leather gloves with three sewn ridges on the back of each hand. You've got a sandwich wrapped in paper tied with twine for the top of the Alp and brandy in a flask for when you get to the bottom, where it's colder. That's the kind of coat you have on.)

Today we're walking in the city. There are window shoppers and tourists. There are wealthy women with six bags each. There are kids getting off a bus. There are businessmen. There's a man selling cups of coffee and I buy us one to share. We sit on a stoop.

Sky: blue and dry. Frozen stone; trees black; our breath white. Smoke. Birds. Air. Stone. Ice. Ground glows with freezing cold and light.

You kiss me, and you can taste the coffee and your happiness.

3.

Now I'm back home. It's five-thirty in the afternoon. Already dark.

I don't want to, but I turn on the TV. Absolutely nothing on. Three kinds of news. Game shows. Re-runs, big sitcom living rooms. Baseball. Teen lifeguards. Cooking in Spanish. *I watch for four and a half hours.*

Now I'm really hungry so I go to the fridge. There's an onion, and a bunch of grapes in a bowl and milk and leftover Vindaloo in a paper carton and mint Milanos and a diet Coke and some more grapes that dropped onto the bottom shelf of the fridge. *I eat everything.*

I'm bored and if I turn the TV on again I'll probably die instantly so I run downstairs to the newsstand on the corner and I buy *Mirabella, Newsweek, Esquire, Vogue, Photo, Interview, Cahiers du Cinema, The Nation, The New Republic, People* and *Us, Details, The Economist, Sassy,* another *Newsweek* since I forgot I already had one on the bottom of my pile, and *Elle. I read them all.*

Now it's five o'clock in the morning and I'm dead tired so I get in bed.

At five-thirty I wake up. I'm fully awake. I get up, pull a sweater on over my nightgown. Thick wool socks and boots. Hat. Put my coat on and walk outside. For a while it's so cold I can't breathe and the wind hurts my face. But after an hour or so I get used to it. And it starts to get light. And I mean this when I say I really do begin to feel better.

ARE YOU READY?

ARE YOU READY? was first produced at the Westbank Theater in New York City January 29, 2001. It was directed by Carl Forsman. The cast was as follows:

MAN .... Ben Shenkman
WOMAN .... Seanna Kofed
MAITRE D' .... Brennan Brown

ARE YOU READY?

*A tableau: Man and Woman standing apart, each waiting
for a table. Maitre d' standing nearby. Man stares at the
woman.*

MAN. Can I kiss you?

WOMAN. Yes!

MAN. *(To us:)* Just like that. I couldn't believe it. I couldn't believe
I *said* it. It was maybe the single bravest thing I'd ever done, but
thought, *I don't care* what — I was in that kind of mood, maybe
you've experienced it? where everything else in the day had been so
awful that you're in the position of saying, What could be worse?
And even feeling a little reckless, like why not give a total stranger
the opportunity to slap me in a crowded restaurant? That would
be the perfect end to this very *bad* day — well, "day" — *week* —
It hadn't been a good *year*, basically — I mean actually I had begun
to question the whole period of the 1990s. 1987 was a good year
for me. But ever since then there had been a series of — I bought
a bagel in a deli in August of 1986 and the cream cheese was a little "off" — not *bad*, not like I wasn't going to eat it, but it didn't
taste quite right, and I think it started there. The next week I quit
my job. Well, "quit" — they gave me — I was *given* the "opportunity" to quit, was how they — I was *fired*, all right, but it was
clearly unfair because how can one person be responsible for the
collapse of an entire Wall Street brokerage house? Right: it makes
no sense. Yes, I made *mistakes* and I could have made some deci-
sions differently that might have saved the company and avoided
touching off Black Monday of 1987, but hindsight is — And in
some ways yes it *was* an opportunity, it was a chance to start over
with a new uh career, and a new *city*, and a new room in my parents' house — because they had redone my old room, they threw
out the bunk beds shaped like a choo-choo train, which was good!

Because my wife would never had stayed there with me if they — that is, she never would have stayed *as long*. Because she had — *we* decided eventually that she had some personal growing left to — and we thought a trial separation would be — she met a Olympic skier from Norway named Kurt, basically, was the deal, and that was great for her, and for our two kids, Jamie and Karen, who live in Oslo now, and they're happy, they love the fjords, and — do you want to see some pictures? They have gotten so big, you wouldn't believe it! I can't — I haven't actually seen them in person since I got out of prison six months ago for embezzlement from the Burger King I was assistant managing while I was living with my parents during the early nineties but I was *totally* innocent, it was the *manager* of the restaurant who was the guilty party and it's complicated but it turns out it's extremely easy for senior management to get away with anything, really, and pin it on an assistant, it has to do with the way Burger King does its bookkeeping, you're probably not interested in that, but anyway it was minimum security, you could play tennis, it was upstate and the leaves in autumn were just *gorgeous* — and just let me show you those pictures: these kids are wonderful. I've got some right here. Let me — No, shit, I forgot: my wallet was stolen on the street this afternoon, just vanished. All my credit cards, my ATM card, everything I had, basically. Gone. *(Beat.)* But I had just taken out 200 dollars in cash: I had that in my pocket. So I was standing there on the street with the money. I thought, I'm thirty-five years old. My family is gone. My career is gone. My wallet is gone. But I have ten twenty-dollar bills in my pocket. And I'm wearing a suit. And I am going to go out tonight to the best restaurant I can find, and eat a decent meal. I deserve at least that. And that's why I came here. And then I saw her. And that's when I said what I said, and that's when she, unbelievably, incredibly, miraculously, said — *(Back to the Tableau:)*

MAITRE D'. Are you ready?

MAN. Can I kiss you?

MAITRE D'. *(To us:)* His table was ready, and I wanted to take him to his table. Does anyone here enjoy a good meal? Could we see a show of hands? "I enjoy a good meal"? Wonderful, thank you. Now, I know what you are thinking. For example this gentleman here, I don't mean to single you out, sir, but I suspect this man here is turning to his not-unattractive companion there and saying with a kind of smirk on his face, "What a idiotic question, who doesn't enjoy a good meal?" While all the time imagining, in all likelihood, something like a Turkeyburger with fries and maybe some cheese or guacamole slopped on top of it for "flavor" — is that about right, sir? How does that sound? Pretty tasty, huh? Well *get out of here you fi'thy bastard* is what I would say to you if I were running this theater now and it were not a theater but a restaurant, because I do not run that kind of restaurant. "What kind of restaurant do you run?" is probably the question you are asking now if you are not already leaving. It's a good question. I think I can answer it best with the following description of how you would go about booking a table at my restaurant in the unlikely event you decided you could afford to eat here. First you should look at a calendar and determine today's date. Then you should pick the date when you would like to have your meal. Now you should do a little math and make sure that the two dates are at least eighteen months apart. Okay? So far so good. Now for the rather more challenging part: you must ask yourself: Am I a major world-class celebrity on the order of, say, Michael Jordan, Mikhail Gorbachev, or Michael Flately, Lord of the Dance? Because if you are not you are just fucked and you are not going to get a table. Except, except, except. There are always exceptions ... *(Softly.)* A couple of nights a year, no more than one or two, when through some random, catastrophic, essentially unknowable chain of events, for a few moment a table lies open. Empty. Its white table-cloth glowing like a beacon of longing and virginal purity in the otherwise absolutely packed dining room. Should you happen to walk in during this fleeting moment of opportunity, and should you happen to be reasonably well dressed, and should you be carrying *cash*, you might find that you are approached by me and offered — now get down on your hands and knees and sing praises to whatever miserable God your fathers prayed to — a table. And when I offer you that table your response must be unequivocal, simple and swift. It must be *yes*. If you hesitate, you are foolish. If you attempt conversation, you will be rebuffed. *And if* you were *insane* enough to say something to me like "can I kiss you," not only would I not even bother to scream *no you cannot kiss me get out of my restaurant you fucking lunatic,* but I would look immediately past you to the person next in line and you would be lost lost lost lost lost. *(Back to the Tableau:)* Are you ready?

WOMAN. Yes! *(To us:)* Thank God. I was hungry. Also, I'm the food critic for the *Times,* and I've been anxious for some time now to get my claws into the throat of that *pompous evil weasel* of a restaurateur and rip him to absolute shreds for the benefit of my rather unusually loyal readership. I'm sorry. I'm not a vindictive person; I think I'm basically a decent person but I'd been watching people humiliating themselves for a table at that place for months, and the restaurant *sucks,* honestly: their foie gras is dry, their lapin en croute a l'Aubergine tastes like something my cat coughed up when it had the flu last winter, their wine list is emaciated, their syphilitic pastry chef couldn't frost a cupcake if you held a gun to his mother's head ... I'd been *dying* to get a crack at it but they wouldn't let me in, not even with a fake name. But tonight I was just walking by and I saw this nice-looking guy, just normal-looking, not a big celeb or anything — he was waiting for a table, so I thought, Why not me? Then I was offered a table and I *leaped* at it and now that supercilious creep is going to have a nasty surprise when he opens the paper tomorrow morning, I promise you. That does sound vindictive, doesn't it? I don't mean it to. I'm not a mean person. I'm just like anyone else. I like a decent meal. I like to rent a couple of videos and relax on a Sunday night. I like to drive up north for a weekend in the fall when the leaves start to turn. That sounds like a horrible personal ad, doesn't it? "Single Female, thirties, enjoys food, film and foliage, seeks single male twenties-thirties for profound lifelong commitment" — Not that I'd ever *ever* write an ad like that — I'm not *desperate,* believe me, I'm *fine.* But all right, yes, I'd like to meet someone, I'd — I mean I *meet* plenty of people, At parties, or — Plenty of successful, brilliant, witty people — all right not plenty but some — and you try to be — but you know people get the paper, they read your stuff and you develop a reputation and even though you're just doing your job — like last month when I wrote that that new *unbelievably* expensive and pretentious sushi place downtown was enough to make an American feel a little less guilty about drop-

72

ping the atomic bomb on Nagasaki — you can develop a reputation for, I don't know, harshness. And you start to wish you could make a clean break. You imagine what it would be like to meet someone totally *new* — like, I don't know, *anyone* — this guy here — just an attractive, well-dressed — I mean I'm not crazy about the tie, frankly, I would have gone with something a little less late-mid-eighties, but who cares? Doesn't matter. You have to be *flexible*. And you have to be ready: you couldn't plan it or hope for it. You would simply have to be prepared to recognize your chance when it came. When that person came along. I sometimes imagine something like that happening. Then I come to my senses and remind myself how unlikely it would be. *(Beat. Back to the Tableau. And now we see the whole sequence again:)*

MAITRE D'. *(To Man.)* Are you ready?

MAN. *(To Woman.)* Can I kiss you?

WOMAN. *(To Maitre d'.)* Yes! *(The maitre d' glares at the man and gestures for the woman to follow him. The woman hasn't heard the man. She follows the maitre d' off. The man watches them go.)*

Blackout

WHAT DO YOU BELIEVE ABOUT THE FUTURE?

WHAT DO YOU BELIEVE ABOUT THE FUTURE? was first produced at the Middlebury College Department of Theater in Middlebury, Vermont, on November 8, 1997. It was directed by Carl Forsman. The cast was as follows: Barry Nelson, Justin Martin, Rich Price, Alex Loth, Aaron Nicholson, Julie Culver, Kelly Dane, Gabrielle Zwain, Kate Michelsen, Laura Beiles.

WHAT DO YOU BELIEVE
ABOUT THE FUTURE?

1. I believe that the United States will cease to exist as a country in my lifetime.
2. Really?
1. Sure. It's too big. It'll break up. In my lifetime. There'll be pieces. The … Republic of Seattle.
2. All right. I believe men and women will walk on the surface of Mars.
1. When?
2. In our lifetime. We will see it happen.
3. I believe that *we* will walk on the surface of Mars.
1. Us?
3. Us personally, us.
1. No.
2. No chance.
3. I believe it's possible. I believe it's possible cars will eventually be phased out.
1. And replaced with what?
3. Some kind of train.
2. Are you out of your mind? There are always going to be cars. Always. We love cars. They're the best. No one is going to ride in a train ever.
3. What if it hovers?
2. So what?
1. Who cares if it hovers?
3. I think it might be neat.
4. Hovering car.
3. What?
4. If you can get a train to hover you sure as hell can get a little car to hover.
1. Yeah, flying car!

3. I believe that in the future there will be trains that hover and —

2. Shut up.

1. Tell us more about the flying car!

4. The flying car will have a backseat like you won't believe. Hit a button and it reclines. Put in a quarter and it vibrates. Put in a *dollar,* and the back seat lifts and arches and curves and wraps itself around you and whomever you happened to invite to join you in the back seat of the flying car that evening. And vibrates and hums. Plus, you're hovering. All over the country, the flying car will radically alter high-school make-out rituals.

1. There won't be a country.

4. Whatever. The People's Republic of Utah. *(Beat.)*

5. I believe that on New Year's Eve, 1999, there will be a rash of suicides. Thousands of suicides all around the world, maybe millions. A global epidemic of panic and mass despair. Not the religious nuts. Not the cults getting ready for the End. Just people in cities who didn't get invited to a good party. *(Beat.)*

6. I believe vegetables will become much better.

1. How do you mean?

6. Better. More satisfying. Richer. Tomatoes like candy. Oranges so orange it hurts to look at them. Corn, ears of sweet corn with only three or four kernels per ear, but huge, swollen, bursting. Mighty broccoli like oak trees, providing shelter *and* nutrition. Fragrant lettuce. We'll all be vegetarians. Steak will come to seem bland and tasteless. Chicken, forget about it. We'll let the chickens go. Chickens will fly free again. They'll be wild birds, like eagles. Vacationing families, fathers on hikes with their children will stop and point up in the sky: "Look kids! A chicken!" *(Beat.)*

3. Hovering boat.

2. What?

3. What about a hovering boat?

2. What about it?

3. I believe it would be neat.

2. Why are you so into this "hovering" thing?

3. It's very futuristic.

2. Who cares if it hovers?

4. A hovering boat. *Come on.*

3. I'm just saying I believe that in the future —

1. You're nuts and you already had your turn. The Greater Indiana-Ohio-Illinois Alliance.

5. In the future, sex will become extremely boring. All of the inhibitions will be broken through. Every taboo overturned, every vestige of hypocrisy totally eliminated. They'll show porn on PBS with the story parts cut out — just the fucking. "Tonight on Masterpiece Theater: *Girls on Girls 24*." At election time the President's intern and the intern of his opponent will go before the voters to contrast their blow-job techniques. Tupperware will make dildos and housewives will hold parties to demonstrate the Anal Intruder. Girl Scouts will go door to door selling condoms in every flavor, including Thin Mint. The backlash, when it comes, will be subtle. Some frat boys gathering in secret late at night to read Jane Austen. Celebrities concealing from the paparazzi their stable, long-term monogamous relationships. And a radical subculture of the kinkiest couples resorting to sex only when they're really, really attracted to someone.

1. The Independent City-State of Orlando, Florida, a wholly-owned subsidiary of the Walt Disney Corporation.

3. I believe that —

1, 2, and 4. Shut up.

7. I believe that the madness of environmental devastation will continue. I believe that the tropical rainforests, and the jungles, and wetlands, and American redwoods that have stood since the time of Christ will continue to fall to the axe and chainsaw. And the rivers will cloud with silt and overflow their banks and then run dry. And more and more species of birds and frogs and elephants and owls and tigers and whales and bears and insects will perish from the earth. And the surface of the earth will grow hot. And the small hole over Antarctica in the earth's protective ozone layer will widen and spread, until the loss of the protective ozone and our resulting continual exposure to intense ultraviolet radiation, combined with widespread intermarriage and the subsequent boom in biracial births, will end ethnic rivalries and racial hatred by producing a human race whose skin the world over is the color of a General Foods International Coffee. *(Beat.)*

8. I believe that I will get a date. *(Beat.)*

9. I believe in the future there will be no television. I believe there

will be no radio. There will be no movies. In the future the internet will not exist. There will be no books, magazines or periodicals. There will be no professional or amateur sports. Fishing, hunting, camping, golfing, biking, hiking, boating, skiing, horseback riding, climbing, swimming? No. There will be no scavenger hunts. There will be no music, live or recorded. There will be no travel for pleasure, no dinner parties. No dancing. No conversation. No arguments. No sex, no friendship, no love. In the future people will play cards. *(Beat.)*

4. They have hovering boats. They're called hovercrafts.

3. Oh yeah. *(Beat.)*

9. Entire newspapers will be given over to the bridge column.

8. I believe the black-haired girl in line at the burrito place on Seventh avenue who stared at me blankly and then turned away as if I didn't exist when I tried to make polite conversation last Friday will come to feel that she really missed an opportunity.

6. I believe in the future love will not be left to amateurs. The sport will be professionalized. Talented young lovers will be identified at an early age and set apart. They'll be coached and tested. They'll be subjected to a rigorous training regimen: Up at six for wooing. Then three hours of courting, followed by lunch, followed by an hour and a half of fondling, then Arthur Murray dance lessons, then out to the restaurant at eight for candlelit dinner time trials. They'll compete. The strong will receive scholarships and signing bonuses. The weak — the needy, the passive-aggressive, the ones not ready for a commitment — will be cut from the program. At the Olympic level the rewards will be huge. Reebok will cover your dating expenses. Nike will sponsor your orgasm. At the end of the year, the world's two top-seeded lovers, emerging triumphant at the end of a grueling season-long double elimination tournament, will make love on national TV. And the rest of us — the non-competitors, the also-rans, the hackers, the *fans* — will watch from our homes in silent admiration.

5. I believe brightly lit cities will sprawl so far and so wide that no stars will be visible at night anywhere in the world. People will visit planetariums the way we go to museums. On New Year's Eve they'll rent out the planetariums for parties. And the demand will be so great they'll have to print out tickets. You'll wait in line for

your allotted time. Of course you'll want to be there right at midnight. Everyone will. So every ticket will say MIDNIGHT. Let's say you don't get in until four in the afternoon on January first. That's okay. It's a planetarium. It's dark. You drink your complimentary glass of champagne. Your ticket says MIDNIGHT. And the stars are positioned exactly where they would be for you at midnight on New Year's Eve if the stars were still visible from earth.

6. Celery ... so ... crisp ...

2. Rainy Martian afternoons.

6. Apples like caramel-covered apples. Corn like candy corn.

8. I will run into that black haired girl sometime on the street and be so ... fucking ... *charming* ...

3. I believe, Goddamn it I believe that bicycles will hover. *(Beat.)*

10. I believe tomorrow morning I will wake up too early. *(Beat.)* I will be half asleep and bleary and I'll get in the shower like I always do, automatically, and stand under the water for a while, and get out and dry off and get dressed, put the coffee on, sit down at the table and drink it. It will not be until halfway through the cup that I will realize my mistake. It's four-thirty in the morning. I don't have to be up for three hours. I didn't look at the clock. I could have kept on sleeping. Now what do I do? I'm dressed. I'm ready to go to work. I'm wide awake. I believe I will not go back to bed. I believe I will stay awake. I believe I'll sit at the table. I believe tomorrow morning I will say to myself, well. It was an accident, but you've done something. You have stolen three hours out of the future. Now they're yours. Now you should sit here with your coffee and look at them a while.

End

WE HAD A VERY
GOOD TIME

CHARACTERS

PAUL, DIMA, men, played by the same actor.

NICOLE, ANNA, women, played by the same actor.

SETTING

Various locations in a foreign country.

WE HAD A VERY GOOD TIME

Scene 1

Paul and Nicole. Each has a paperback book.

NICOLE. "The cathedral is one of the largest in all of Europe. Though completely destroyed during the war, it was rebuilt in the 1950s with funds raised by the order of Carmelite nuns who operate the brewery next door."
PAUL. Cathedral.
NICOLE. We haven't seen this one.
PAUL. No. *(Beat.)*
NICOLE. "Be sure to spend at least two and a half hours wandering in the gardens that abut the reliquary. Mercenaries imprisoned here in the 1840s planted the yew trees and crafted the famous miniature topiary bulldogs that 'guard' the entrance to the gift shop and restrooms."
PAUL. We're here, it's here.
NICOLE. I think it will be interesting. *(Beat.)*
PAUL. Let's get breakfast.
NICOLE. It says to get here early.
PAUL. We should eat. *(Beat.)*
NICOLE. We could get something.
PAUL. I mean *breakfast*. Not a cup of coffee and a roll.
NICOLE. It's a continental breakfast.
PAUL. It's not enough. I want eggs.
NICOLE. Where is the water?
PAUL. You've got it. And I want a second cup of coffee.
NICOLE. You can get anything you want. Did you forget the water?
PAUL. Honey, you put it in your bag.

85

NICOLE. *Paul … (He turns her around and digs in her backpack. He produces a water bottle.)* "A donation of fourteen-twenty is required by the Carmelite order, but the views of the beer garden alone are worth it, especially after sunset." *(Drinks.)* Maybe we shouldn't see this now. "At sunset, here, in the late summer weeks, the great fiery ball of the sun can be seen to slip majestically out of view just behind the oval limestone sculpture built in 1974 to celebrate the achievements of the nation's textile workers." *(Paul is looking at a phrase book.)*

PAUL. How do you say, I'd like some more coffee please?

NICOLE. I don't know.

PAUL. Well I don't know what we're supposed to do until tonight. We should probably plan to be indoors.

NICOLE. Why?

PAUL. Look at the sky. It looks murderous.

NICOLE. Oh don't rain. Don't rain. Don't rain.

PAUL. Hey, look, if it —

NICOLE. *Don't rain.*

PAUL. It's okay if it rains. It —

NICOLE. On our last day.

PAUL. Look, if it rains we'll just go to a movie or something.

NICOLE. A *movie?*

PAUL. Sure.

NICOLE. We can see movies at home. I'll find something.

PAUL. Two weeks, maybe we've seen everything.

NICOLE. In the *country?*

PAUL. It's a small country.

NICOLE. Are you out of your mind?

PAUL. *(Trying out phrases.)* "Hello." "Good morning." "You do not seem to understand, my wife and I are very hungry."

NICOLE. What about art?

PAUL. I thought we saw it.

NICOLE. We saw the national museum and the national *crafts* museum and the city museum. There's more. Here. *(She studies.)*

PAUL. *(Flipping through the phrase book.)* "Can you direct me to the hotel?" "Can you direct me to the train station?" "We have become separated from our group." "We have lost our luggage." "We have lost our tickets." "I have lost my passport." "I have lost

86

my umbrella." "I cannot find my husband/wife." God, this is *depressing.* "I would like to speak to the maitre d'hotel. I would like to speak to the manager. This mattress is uncomfortable. This room has no windows. This meal is unsatisfactory. This soup is cold. Tell the cook I would like to have a word with him." What an asshole. Listen to this, if you only read the English it's like the rantings of a lunatic: "We have lost our maps. We are out of gas. We have a flat tire. Please call a mechanic. No, that is too expensive. This man is not trustworthy. Very well I will change the tire myself. Help me, I have hurt my back. My wife will change the tire. Please call the police! My wife's necklace has been stolen! My wallet/watch/cigarette case is missing! Where is the hospital? My husband/wife is very ill! My husband/wife requires a blood transfusion! I need to speak to the embassy! Get me the ambassador!"

NICOLE. *Stop it!*

PAUL. I'm just reading the —

NICOLE. I don't like it.

PAUL. Sorry.

NICOLE. Listen, this sounds *wonderful:* "En route to the porcelain factory, be sure to make time for the much smaller, less magnificent, more recent, but nonetheless noteworthy Church of the Six Apostles. Though completely bombed out of existence during the War it was rebuilt in 1978 by funds collected by the ecclesiastical authorities from third-world schoolchildren."

PAUL. I propose we adopt a strict "no cathedrals" policy for the rest of the trip.

NICOLE. This is a *church.* Let's do it, then we'll have breakfast outside in a cafe.

PAUL. Okay.

NICOLE. Really?

PAUL. It sounds interesting.

NICOLE. I think it will be. We're still here.

PAUL. I know.

NICOLE. I get the feeling that mentally you're halfway home already.

PAUL. No.

NICOLE. Worrying about packing. How to get to the airport.

PAUL. I'm not.

NICOLE. Good. Don't, not yet.

PAUL. The last place I want to be —

NICOLE. Me too!

PAUL. Is back home, so —

NICOLE. So let's enjoy what we —

PAUL. I think we're both — yes. *Yes.*

NICOLE. All right. *(Beat.)* There's the sun!

PAUL. Yeah.

NICOLE. Did you bring my sunglasses?

PAUL. They're in your bag, Nicole.

NICOLE. No. You —

PAUL. Ugh. Just — *(He digs in her backpack.)* Where are the passports?

NICOLE. They're —

PAUL. I told you not to leave them in the hotel room.

NICOLE. I've got them in my jacket, Paul.

PAUL. Are you sure?

NICOLE. They're right here with the plane tickets, okay?

PAUL. Do you want me to carry them?

NICOLE. No! I've got them.

PAUL. Well I don't see the sunglasses.

NICOLE. Here. I'm sure you — *(She digs in his backpack.)*

PAUL. What are you doing?

NICOLE. See? Okay? Everything's here. *(She produces the glasses and they put them on.)* Let's go home with sunburns. Mm. Water?

PAUL. Okay. *(They drink bottled water.)* The Church of the *Six* Apostles.

NICOLE. Yes.

PAUL. We've been there.

NICOLE. No.

PAUL. Last week. It was the horrible place with the corrugated iron roof and the crucifix made of —

NICOLE. Oh God, you're right. "En route to the porcelain factory."

PAUL. You bought too much porcelain.

NICOLE. Well, we can give it as gifts. All right: "For the first time pleasure traveler and the jaded junketeer alike, this beautiful country offers a seemingly endless array of pleasures" —

PAUL. All of which we've seen.

NICOLE. Don't. You've had a good time.

PAUL. Yes.

NICOLE. We've been together.

PAUL. That has been the best part.

NICOLE. For me too. We've needed this.

PAUL. I know.

NICOLE. Not just a vacation, but an opportunity —

PAUL. Yes.

NICOLE. To to re-, to re- ...

PAUL. ... -ignite?

NICOLE. Re*store* everything that —

PAUL. Honey, yes. Yes.

NICOLE. Let me have the water. *(Drinks.)* And step away from everything at home ... what time is it at home?

PAUL. Maybe three or four in the morning.

NICOLE. God I love it: at home people are in bed in their cold and boring bedrooms and we're here standing in the sun in this beautiful country. It's a beautiful country.

PAUL. It's very nice.

NICOLE. You don't need a book to tell you. And when you think what this country's been through.

PAUL. Yes.

NICOLE. Even in just the last forty years. In the last *ten* years.

PAUL. It's amazing that it's —

NICOLE. The people have this amazing spirit.

PAUL. They're very nice people.

NICOLE. Especially, with the upheavals, I mean, the uncertainty and the economic stress and the political transition ...

PAUL. They're very nice.

NICOLE. It's amazing they're as nice as they are. Like the man at the airport. And when you think that we have so *much*, it's really disgusting. Not *us* us but as a nation — The food, the unbelievable amounts of food, the cars, the clothes. You go into a grocery store and there are acres of vegetables, meat, fish, God the meat at home, it's bright red and *pulsating* there's so much of it in the coolers at the grocery, and cans of soup — *condiments* — the mustards, different sizes of pickles, thirty-five kinds of ketchup, I mean, the extravagance of that. That we live in a society that's developed to

89

the point where we have the resources for that kind of variety and amount of ketchup to be created and transported and displayed, so that it's within the reach of, really, anybody, that we can *do* that (all those tomatoes), it's an unbelievable achievement if you think about it, historically, and yet, I mean, who needs those kinds of condiments? It's not even really *food.* And yet these people do want it, they envy it, they're dying for it, they risk their lives, torture — they have revolutions, overthrow *governments* for it.

PAUL. What man at the airport? *(Beat. Sky darkens. Nicole takes off her sunglasses.)*

NICOLE. Oh no.

PAUL. What?

NICOLE. Did you feel that?

PAUL. No, what? *(It's very dark. Thunder.)*

NICOLE. Did you bring the umbrella? *(Paul reaches for the phrasebook. He reads.)*

PAUL. "We have lost our umbrella ... "

NICOLE. STOP IT.

PAUL. "We need to speak to the ambassador ... "

NICOLE. Knock it off. What are we supposed to do?

PAUL. I don't know. *(They take off their coats, cover their heads, run a few steps to some temporary shelter from the rain.)*

NICOLE. Shut up. Listen. "On rainy days the intimate and unpopular Museum of Discarded Craftwork (located just a few kilometers off the town square) is a perfect hideaway ... Featuring ironwork, stone carvings, and portions of frescoes salvaged from area churches following their destruction in the War ... well worth two or three hours leisurely exploration ... donations accepted." Well!

PAUL. Do they have movies here?

NICOLE. Yes.

PAUL. Let's go see a movie.

NICOLE. We can see a movie at home, Paul. We're *here,* we —

PAUL. I don't think the criteria should just be, "can we or can we not do this at home."

NICOLE. A movie.

PAUL. Yes. *(Beat. She looks through the book.)*

NICOLE. "Native cinema is flourishing with the recent relaxation of government content restrictions. The National Film Archive has daily screenings of historical epics, ethnographic documentaries, and compilations of the short animated political allegories so popular among radical university students."

PAUL. Nicole, let's find the junkiest, stupidest, loudest American action movie playing and just go and buy two tickets, and a bag of popcorn or barley or small rocks or whatever they serve at the movies here, and just watch it. That's what we'll do.

NICOLE. We're on vacation.

PAUL. Yes, we should have fun. We'll go to a movie. And then we'll find a bar, not a *brewery* in a *barn* run by *nuns,* one of the good hotel bars and we'll sit by the window and I will buy you a drink. And then if it's still raining we will go back to the hotel —

NICOLE. All right —

PAUL. And keep the windows open so we can hear the rain, and get in bed ... *(He kisses her.)* I know we can "do this at home," but ... *(Long kiss.)*

NICOLE. But ...

PAUL. It's different in a foreign country.

NICOLE. Ha. Yes ...

PAUL. Haven't you noticed?

NICOLE. Yes. *(Kiss.)* How, though?

PAUL. Well for one thing the time difference.

NICOLE. Ah.

PAUL. At home it would be the middle of the day.

NICOLE. Yes.

PAUL. And I think you're more relaxed.

NICOLE. Uh huh.

PAUL. I certainly am. *(Kiss.)*

NICOLE. Paul, you're dripping on the book.

PAUL. Don't worry about it.

NICOLE. No, let me —

PAUL. Throw the book away.

NICOLE. Let go.

PAUL. Please. Get rid of it. I mean it.

NICOLE. Stop! I need it.

PAUL. Forget the book! There is nothing left to do here!

NICOLE. We've been here for a week. People live here for decades and —

PAUL. They don't keep up our pace. Three museums a day, churches, markets —

NICOLE. The man at the airport said —

PAUL. What *man* at the *airport?*

NICOLE. He helped me with the luggage — he was *friendly* ... when you were dealing with the passports and the visas. There are nice people. He said explore. He said you can't understand the country unless you explore. He sold me the guidebook. He said this country would reveal itself to certain people if they were patient and fearless enough.

PAUL. I think we've been quite patient with this country.

NICOLE. What will happen when we get home? When you go back to work and I go back to work —

PAUL. We'll be relaxed.

NICOLE. I don't want to be *relaxed.*

PAUL. When we get home —

NICOLE. *I don't want to go home. (Beat.)*

PAUL. Honey, we're wet and hungry. Let's —

NICOLE. Don't touch me. *(Beat.)* Do you want to open the mail?

PAUL. What?

NICOLE. When I think about opening the mail ... And going through the papers. And listening to one two three four nineteen twenty messages on the machine. And calling back our fucking friends —

PAUL. Nicole.

NICOLE. And living with you in that apartment. *(Beat.)* I'm sorry, could I have the water? *(He gives it to her. She drinks. She gets out the book.)* "Connoisseurs of agricultural equipment will find much to interest them at the large area behind the low-income housing projects next to the river. There, discarded harvesters left over from the days of forced collectivization have been left to rust in the open air, producing a delightfully unpretentious impromptu sculpture garden." *(Beat.)* That sounds ...

PAUL. Nicole ... *(Beat. He tries to take the book. She holds on to it. He pulls harder. She resists. The book's cover rips and it drops to the ground.)*

NICOLE. Look what you've done. *(She picks it up. A piece of paper flutters out. She looks at it. She picks it up. Beat.)* "Private tours. See the city. By arrangement." And a number.

PAUL. Nicole.

NICOLE. Let's call.

PAUL. Come on.

NICOLE. Paul.

PAUL. It's our last afternoon.

NICOLE. Yes.

PAUL. You're going to run all over looking for some scam artist who —

NICOLE. I knew you would say that. I knew you would say that.

PAUL. A guy at the *airport.*

NICOLE. I think we should at least *try* to —

PAUL. If you fall for this —

NICOLE. "Fall"?

PAUL. The way you fell for the porcelain factory and the iron workers hall of fame and the concrete museum and the free patriotic *puppet* shows, and the crippled children playing *basketball* ...

NICOLE. *All right.*

PAUL. I mean how much disappointment can one person take?

NICOLE. Are you disappointed?

PAUL. Yes. *(Beat.)*

NICOLE. I'm gonna call.

PAUL. Nicole. *(She exits.)* Nicole. *(Beat. He gets out the phrasebook.)* "I would like to see a film." "Can you direct me to the nearest cinema?" "Can you direct me to the hotel?" "Can you direct me to the train station?" "We have lost our luggage." "We have lost our tickets." "I have lost my passport." "I have lost my umbrella." "I have lost my husband/wife."

Scene 2

Nicole and Dima.

NICOLE. Hello.
DIMA. Hello. I'm Dima.
NICOLE. Nicole.
DIMA. Very glad to see you again Nicole.
NICOLE. Thank you.
DIMA. You still have the book.
NICOLE. That's how I got your number.
DIMA. I hope it has been useful.
NICOLE. We've used it every day.
DIMA. Good. *(Beat.)*
NICOLE. When does the tour start?
DIMA. Now. If you like.
NICOLE. Oh! All right.
DIMA. Good.
NICOLE. Do we start here?
DIMA. We can start anywhere you'd like.
NICOLE. Where do we meet the other people?
DIMA. You're the only one.
NICOLE. It's just me?
DIMA. You're the only one who called. *(Beat.)*
NICOLE. How much will this cost?
DIMA. Whatever you like.
NICOLE. I don't understand.
DIMA. You pay what you like.
NICOLE. I think we should agree on a figure before we start.
DIMA. I show you the city, you pay me what you think it was worth.
NICOLE. What if I don't like the tour?
DIMA. You pay me nothing.
NICOLE. Not very economical for you.

DIMA. No.

NICOLE. Good deal for me, though.

DIMA. You lose an afternoon. *(Beat.)*

NICOLE. Let's do it.

DIMA. Yes?

NICOLE. Yes. We start here?

DIMA. If you like.

NICOLE. I like.

DIMA. Good.

NICOLE. Good! How long will the whole thing take?

DIMA. As long as you —

NICOLE. Dima. Come on now, let's nail something down.

DIMA. How long does it take to see a city? An afternoon? A lifetime?

NICOLE. How do you make any money?

DIMA. Money. Do we have to talk about money?

NICOLE. I'd like to know how much all this will cost.

DIMA. *I hate money.*

NICOLE. Oh.

DIMA. You probably find that hard to believe.

NICOLE. No.

DIMA. You people in the West love money.

NICOLE. I think we're ambivalent.

DIMA. I don't care about money.

NICOLE. Now which is it?

DIMA. What?

NICOLE. Do you hate it or do you not care?

DIMA. Both.

NICOLE. Well if you hate it you obviously care about it.

DIMA. I hate what it's done to my country and I care about my country.

NICOLE. What has it done?

DIMA. Fast food. Mafia killing. Health clubs.

NICOLE. What did you have before? Poverty.

DIMA. We still have poverty but when everyone was poor we cared about freedom and literature and poetry. Now some people are driving around in Mercedes and no one reads.

NICOLE. Do you wish it could be the way it was before?

DIMA. The old system?

NICOLE. Yes.

DIMA. No. It was inhuman.

NICOLE. So what's the solution?

DIMA. The solution? I don't know what is the solution. Why are you asking me? I'm a tour guide.

NICOLE. You know what I'd like? Show me the places where the revolution happened. Could you do a tour like that?

DIMA. A revolutionary tour?

NICOLE. Yes. Do you know any of the places?

DIMA. Yes.

NICOLE. Great. I'll pay you whatever you think it's worth.

DIMA. I will accept only what *you* think it is worth.

NICOLE. Fine. Great.

DIMA. If it is worth nothing, you pay nothing.

NICOLE. Sounds fair.

DIMA. If you like the tour, if you do think it is worth something, what I give to you —

NICOLE. Yes.

DIMA. You pay nothing.

NICOLE. No, Dima …

DIMA. Unless you absolutely feel it is really worth something, and then you give me only what you think it is worth.

NICOLE. Deal.

DIMA. Less, if you want. I hate this money, greed, the market, talking about prices: it makes me uncomfortable.

NICOLE. I can see that. Relax, we'll work it out. Should we go?

DIMA. Yes, okay.

NICOLE. Where is our first historic spot?

DIMA. You are standing in one now. (*Beat. She looks around. She consults the book.*)

NICOLE. "This out-of-the-way plaza, historically the center of the city's ball-bearing industry, suffered extensive bombing damage during the war, and is now used mainly as a staging area for patriotic military parades."

DIMA. That book is out of date.

NICOLE. You sold me this book.

DIMA. It predates the revolution.

96

NICOLE. What happened here?

DIMA. The tanks were coming down the avenue there. It was the main route to the parliament so people built barricades to keep them back. So the tanks turned the corner there, and cut through here, where there were no barricades and they could fire on the parliament buildings.

NICOLE. So what happened?

DIMA. Some people on the barricades on the avenue realized what was going on. They ran over here, a dozen of them. The tanks were just turning the corner into this plaza. It was midnight, very dark, August first, a hot night. No moon; the demonstrators carried flashlights. They didn't have weapons. A couple had Molotov cocktails but these are useless unless the tanks are open and besides these are our people driving the tanks. A couple dozen more people had arrived: as many as could leave the barricade on the avenue. They lay down on the pavement. Stretched out — spread their arms and legs wide: there were just enough people to do this and reach all the way across the plaza with their fingertips touching. They were lying there in the path of the tanks. Staring straight up at the sky: no moon, no stars, cloudy night. It was humid. The tanks had to stop. That was the idea — that the boys driving the tanks would not drive over their brothers, cousins, classmates, their girlfriends in the street. The tanks stopped. For a minute no one knew what to do. Everyone was lying there. The pavement was very uncomfortable. Then one of the protesters stood up. He shouted at the tanks. "Soldiers! Remember that you have taken an oath to your country. Your weapons cannot be turned against the people! Clouds of terror and dictatorship are gathering over us but this night will not be eternal and our long-suffering people will find freedom once again, and forever. Soldiers! I believe at this fateful hour you will make the right decision. The honor of our country will not be covered with the blood of the people. Join us." Everyone was waiting. Then the top of one tank opened and a soldier popped his head out. He looked very small. He had a rifle and he threw it to the pavement. Everyone leaped up. Everyone cheered. The other tanks opened. The soldiers poured out of the hatches. They threw away their guns. They were dancing on top of the tanks. Girls climbed up on the tanks and kissed the soldiers. We swarmed around the tanks. One soldier had a tape deck. He turned it on full blast. The Beatles singing "Twist and Shout." Everyone was dancing, kissing, crying. It happened right here.

NICOLE. Were you here?

DIMA. Yes.

NICOLE. Was it you who shouted at the tanks?

DIMA. No. I couldn't have done that. I'm not … articulate.

NICOLE. You are.

DIMA. Not articulate. Sorry, my English. I mean … We were terrified. No one knew what would happen. I thought maybe I am about to die. Or throw up. My skin was cold. I was glad I was lying on the pavement in case I fainted. I couldn't speak. Someone else did, someone who wasn't afraid.

NICOLE. I'm sure they were afraid too.

DIMA. Someone who could speak while afraid. Is there a word for that?

NICOLE. I don't know. I don't think so.

DIMA. Sorry. My English —

NICOLE. — is excellent.

DIMA. No.

NICOLE. It is.

DIMA. There are so many things I can't say.

NICOLE. Like what?

DIMA. Well that's the problem, I can't say them —

NICOLE. No, no, of course. *(Beat.)*

DIMA. Anyway, all that was ten years ago. I was a kid.

NICOLE. You were brave. *(Beat.)*

DIMA. Where is your husband? At the airport I saw you with …

NICOLE. I don't know. I mean we decided to do separate things.

DIMA. On your last day?

NICOLE. Yes. *(Beat.)* Where do we go next?

DIMA. There is a place by the river.

NICOLE. The river.

DIMA. Yes.

NICOLE. What happened there?

DIMA. I have a room. *(Beat.)* I'm sorry, my English. I don't mean … I don't mean to suggest … I have said the wrong thing, my

English, excuse me.

NICOLE. It's all right.

DIMA. *(Laughs.)* I think I have suggested an incorrect thing.

NICOLE. *(Laughs.)* I think you have.

DIMA. I'm sorry.

NICOLE. It's okay!

DIMA. I am embarrassed.

NICOLE. Don't be, it's okay, it's a mistake. For a minute I thought ...

DIMA. What?

NICOLE. *(Laughs.)* Well, I thought you were saying we should go back to your room together.

DIMA. For sex.

NICOLE. *(Laughs.)* Yes!

DIMA. That is what I was saying. *(Beat.)*

NICOLE. So why were you apologizing?

DIMA. With my clumsiness, I made it sound like this is a scheduled part of the tour, something we must do, when instead I meant it only as an invitation.

NICOLE. Oh my God.

DIMA. It would be entirely up to you.

NICOLE. Jesus Christ, I don't know you.

DIMA. You can stay as long as you want, or as little as you want. I know this is unusual. This is not typical tour-guide behavior. Or maybe in some countries it is, I don't know.

NICOLE. I am married.

DIMA. You left your husband.

NICOLE. I did not.

DIMA. You're not with him today. You weren't with him at the airport.

NICOLE. Of course I was.

DIMA. No.

NICOLE. You don't know what you're talking about.

DIMA. You weren't *with* him. He was busy, handling your passports, suitcases, visas, money. Rigging, all the rigging.

NICOLE. Rigging?

DIMA. I'm sorry, my English, it's not right. Rigging like a circus.

NICOLE. What? No, I don't —

DIMA. These ropes and lines and nets — what do you call them, then? Rigging. To keep you safe. That's what your husband was doing, installing all of this complicated rigging to prevent your falling too far, too quickly, away from life at home.

NICOLE. Oh, I see ...

DIMA. But I saw you, Nicole. You had already fallen. You had arrived in another place and you were the only one here. *(Beat.)* I intend no disrespect to your husband. I wasn't thinking this at the time. I wasn't thinking about him. I didn't even notice him. I noticed you. It's luck that I met you. I almost never go to the airport. I find customers in town, at the big hotels, the tourists. But it was quiet that day and I couldn't find any tourists so I thought I'd try my luck at the airport. I'm sick of showing the city to tourists, they don't see anything, they look at the city through the viewfinders of their camcorders, they wouldn't even know they'd been here if they could not take home the videotape as evidence. I hate tourists.

NICOLE. I'm a tourist.

DIMA. No. You're a traveler. Tourists worry only about where they're going. Travelers care about where they've been. I didn't expect to see someone like you. I felt lucky just talking to you when you bought the book. I thought about you afterwards. How ... attractive ... you are. I never imagined you'd call. I couldn't believe my luck when you did. I think in speaking to you like this I've made a terrible mistake. *(Beat.)*

NICOLE. It's all right.

DIMA. It's not. I can't forgive myself. I understand if you want to end the tour now.

NICOLE. No. No, of course not.

DIMA. Are you sure?

NICOLE. Yes. We haven't seen anything.

DIMA. I'd love to continue if you are willing.

NICOLE. Yes. We have the whole afternoon.

DIMA. My God I am so relieved. Thanks. Thank you. Yes. Which way do you want to go? Pick a direction.

NICOLE. Well where's the next place of interest?

DIMA. There are places of interest everywhere. We'll find everything interesting. Pick the direction you want to go. *(Beat.)*

NICOLE. Which way is the river?
DIMA. Behind us, there.
NICOLE. How long will it take to walk there?
DIMA. Not long. Not very long. *(Beat.)*
NICOLE. Let's move in that direction.

Scene 3

Anna and Paul, struggling.

ANNA. Let me go!
PAUL. What did you do with it?
ANNA. Stop it!
PAUL. I know you have it.
ANNA. If you don't let go of my arm I'm going to spit in your face you bastard! *Let me go!*
PAUL. All right, listen, let's both just calm down. All right? Stop screaming.
ANNA. *Let me go!*
PAUL. I'm not going to let go.
ANNA. *Let go of my arm goddamn it!*
PAUL. People are staring. Is that what you want? *(He pulls her off to one side.)* I don't want any trouble.
ANNA. Jesus you ugly son of a bitch. You're going to break my wrist.
PAUL. I'm not going to let go so you may as well stop screaming.
ANNA. I don't understand a fucking thing you're saying.
PAUL. Let's take care of this quietly. Just give back the wallet and I'll let you go, all right?
ANNA. Why are you jabbering at me? I don't speak English you fucking idiot.
PAUL. Come on. Let's go. You bumped me and I felt you take it out of my pocket. You screwed up, I caught you. Where is it?
ANNA. ARE YOU INSANE? What are you doing?
PAUL. Stop yelling. Listen to my voice. Listen to my calm voice.

Okay? I'm calm. Let's be calm! Calm. If you give it back I won't call the police. I don't want any hassle. It's my last day here I'd prefer not to spend it in a police station filling out reports. Just give the wallet back and we'll call it a day, all right?

ANNA. Please ...

PAUL. *(Gently.)* Good, take it easy. You seem less upset, great.

ANNA. Wait a minute.

PAUL. Calm. Relax. Good.

ANNA. Why are you speaking that way?

PAUL. Calm.

ANNA. This is disturbing.

PAUL. We understand each other. Do we have a deal? Do you understand?

ANNA. Why are you smiling like that?

PAUL. It's not even the cash, I don't care about that. I know you people need hard currency. It's the credit cards that are a hassle to replace.

ANNA. Oh my God. You're a psychopath.

PAUL. I had a Visa card stolen in Miami two summers ago and it took the company in Denver *six weeks* to send me a replacement.

ANNA. Jesus you're insane. Are you going to rape me? You're going to drag me off, is that it?

PAUL. I was so annoyed I switched to AmEx for a while but you can't use it in as many places and you have to pay the full amount at the end of every billing period.

ANNA. HELP ME! Let me go! You eat shit for lunch and your mother fucks pigs you sick bastard American!

PAUL. "American"? Yes, I'm American! Hi!

ANNA. Please. I'll tell you my name. I've read about this. If I tell you my name you're more likely to see me as a human being, an individual, and you won't hurt me as much. Okay? I'm Anna.

PAUL. Just — What?

ANNA. Please. I'm Anna. My name is Anna.

PAUL. Anna?

ANNA. Yes! Anna.

PAUL. Paul. *(He drops her wrist. He pulls out the phrasebook. She is about to run away when:)*

PAUL. "My name is Paul." *(He looks through the book. Reads:)*

"My wallet has been stolen." "Do you have … my wallet?"

ANNA. What? No! *(Paul consults the book.)*

PAUL. "No." *(Paul looks at her. She looks frightened. He slowly searches his pants pockets. He feels his coat pocket. He pulls out a wallet. Beat.)* I'm sorry. I must have put it in my coat after lunch. I don't usually — it's my mistake, I — *(Searches in the book.)* "I'm sorry."

ANNA. You're SORRY?

PAUL. "I'm sorry."

ANNA. That's great. You could have broken my wrist you stupid son of a bitch!

PAUL. Your wrist? Did I hurt your wrist?

ANNA. You shit-eating bastard! You scared me to death!

PAUL. You must be furious. I'm sorry. "I'm sorry."

ANNA. Ah, you're sorry, you're sorry. To hell with you. Fly back to America and be fucked by stinking men until you are bent double like a monkey. *(She starts off.)*

PAUL. Wait! Anna. Anna! Here. *(He opens his wallet and offers money.)*

ANNA. Oh, money. Terrific. Money will fix everything. You assault me on the street, you nearly break my arm, you put in me the fear of rape and bloody murder and you offer me *money?*

PAUL. I feel awful. Take it, please. Here. *(She takes it contemptuously. Beat.)*

ANNA. A hundred dollars.

PAUL. It's a hundred dollars. *(Consults book.)* "A hundred dollars."

ANNA. I can see.

PAUL. I don't mean to insult you. You can at least get your arm checked out. *(Indicates.)* Your arm? At a doctor. *(Indicates.)* Doctor? Would that be enough?

ANNA. You give a hundred dollars to a stranger on the street.

PAUL. It's probably not enough.

ANNA. A hundred dollars. Just like that! Here, take it.

PAUL. More? Would you need more?

ANNA. I've never seen a hundred dollars. Except in suitcases in movies.

PAUL. You keep saying "a hundred dollars." I don't understand.

ANNA. How much more currency are you willing to part with, my philanthropic friend?

PAUL. Is that not enough?

ANNA. Let's try for another C note, shall we?

PAUL. I'm sorry, I don't understand.

ANNA. Look at my face. Look. I'm weak and impoverished.

PAUL. I don't —

ANNA. Yet noble. Noble. The unquenchable human spirit. See?

PAUL. Jesus I am sorry. I don't know what's wrong with me. I nearly break your arm and I think a hundred will ... Here, take this.

ANNA. A hundred more. You can do better than that. Look at the centuries of exploitation carved into my features.

PAUL. Okay? Is that enough? I don't know what to say. You have to understand I don't usually go around wrestling strange women on the street.

ANNA. You seem contrite. I don't want to push it. Here's the deal: I'll take this gratefully. Quick shy smile for you. See? *(She takes the bill.)* But I'll just let the trace of a shadow of disappointment flicker over my haunted face. Okay? No pressure, ball's in your court. *(Beat. Paul looks in the book.)*

PAUL. "Would you like to see a movie?" *(Anna laughs. For a minute she can't stop laughing. Paul laughs with her.)*

ANNA. "A movie?"

PAUL. Yes! "A movie." Why not, what do you say? It's on me.

ANNA. Yes, I would. I would like to see a movie. In the middle of the day, I love it, take the afternoon off. What an offer! Would you buy me a Coke too?

PAUL. Coke!

ANNA. Coke!

PAUL. You want a Coke? To drink?

ANNA. A Coke! Yes! Popcorn!

PAUL. Pop — Oh, at the movie? Yes, sure, popcorn! Yeah. And I like candy at the movies, Junior Mints — it's the only time I eat them.

ANNA. Popcorn and Coke at a movie! And I'll just skip the rest of the day, not go into work, it's a wonderful idea! And be fired immediately so I can go to see Tom Cruise, and then not be able to pay the rent and be turned out of my apartment and starve.

PAUL. You like Tom Cruise?

ANNA. Tom Cruise, ugh, please, I wouldn't cross the street to see him. He's a poor actor, he's little and he has a shrill voice. I prefer Burt Lancaster. I would be turned out of my apartment for Burt Lancaster. But he's dead so I'm afraid I must go to work.

PAUL. *From Here to Eternity.*

ANNA. What?

PAUL. *From Here (Gestures.) HERE ... to Eternity.* Uh, eternity: *(He flails his arms to indicate the sky, the universe. Beat.)*

ANNA. Ah. Yes, I see. It's a good movie. I've seen it. Lovers kissing on the beach. Black and white. Hawaii. They make love at the shoreline. I like the film. *(Beat.)* You're not a bad man. Are you alone? You're lonely. Are you married? Are you traveling alone? You're probably on business. Far away from home with a wallet full of hundred dollar bills. It's fun to take a trip. We're all lonely. Here. *(She gives his money back.)* Go back to your hotel. There are women there who sleep with lonely businessmen for a lot less than this. I can't go to a movie with you. I have a life. We have nothing in common. *(Beat.)* Don't use those women, all right? Have a drink by yourself. Go to a movie. Fly home and make love to your wife, who probably misses you.

Scene 4

A restaurant. Paul and Nicole. Beat.

PAUL. How is it?

NICOLE. Good. How's yours?

PAUL. Mm. Good. Very good.

NICOLE. Good. You usually order well.

PAUL. More wine?

NICOLE. No. Maybe in a minute. *(Beat.)*

PAUL. I was worried.

NICOLE. Sorry I was late.

PAUL. It's okay. Just didn't want to be up too late, is all. We have to get up early tomorrow. We can sleep on the plane. Get up at maybe six.

NICOLE. Jesus.

PAUL. Okay, if we pack tonight get up at six thirty, then half an hour to get to the airport and we should be there an hour before the flight for passports, luggage, and then we're in the air at nine and that's two a.m. our time, home, so we're really sleeping from maybe, two until nine in the morning at home.

NICOLE. Yes.

PAUL. That's a good night's sleep. That should be fine. And we land and it's nine o'clock and we're rested and the day begins. Drink lots of water ... *(Beat.)*

NICOLE. It's strange.

PAUL. What?

NICOLE. It's better going back. It's easier — with your sleep — if you just sleep going home then the time works out.

PAUL. I don't —

NICOLE. You sleep going home, it's seven hours home and it's seven hours behind, so that works out perfectly.

PAUL. But you sleep coming over.

NICOLE. But you're not going *back*. In *time,* you see? You're going forward, that's what throws you off coming *over,* but going back —

PAUL. No.

NICOLE. Listen to what I'm saying. You lose *no time* going back because the time zones go *backward.*

PAUL. Yes. But that doesn't mean you're not going to be jetlagged when you —

NICOLE. You *just said* we'd get up at nine and be rested and start the day. Did you say that?

PAUL. We *should* start the day to get on the new schedule, but we'll still be — by the *evening* —

NICOLE. We *leave at nine* and fly backwards through *seven time zones* for *seven hours* so we get home *at nine.* It's the *same.*

PAUL. It's not the same! You're going to be lagged! At eleven at night your body will think it's five in the morning.

NICOLE. I'd like some more wine. You don't know what you're saying. You'll have caught up because you *slept while you were on the plane.*

PAUL. You slept going over.

NICOLE. More.

PAUL. Were you jetlagged when you got here?

NICOLE. Listen.

PAUL. *Were you jetlagged* —

NICOLE. Yes, but listen: do you understand that the *earth rotates?* Do you understand that? Only in one direction! It doesn't jiggle back and forth like a bellydancer. So going *home* is in some way different from going *away*. Are you with me?

PAUL. You should watch that. You get more lagged if you drink alcohol, coffee —

NICOLE. *I don't care.*

PAUL. All right. *(Beat.)* How much money do you have left?

NICOLE. None.

PAUL. Really? Nothing?

NICOLE. Nothing.

PAUL. Good. I've got enough to get us to the airport and breakfast.

NICOLE. Okay.

PAUL. Didn't want to change currency back.

NICOLE. Good.

PAUL. You've got nothing?

NICOLE. Nope. *(Beat.)*

PAUL. Anything we should get before we go?

NICOLE. I don't think so.

PAUL. For gifts?

NICOLE. We have the porcelain.

PAUL. Right. Good. So we can give that to your mother, and my Dad, and Frank, and Benjy and Nate, and Sarah and Jackie, and Amanda …

NICOLE. And my boss and your boss.

PAUL. Good. That was a good deal. Good trip. Smart. I'm glad we went to the factory. I'm glad we came here. *(Beat.)* Should I order another bottle?

NICOLE. Do we have the cash?

PAUL. I'll put this on the credit card.

NICOLE. They stick you with the exchange rate.

PAUL. It's our last night. *(Beat.)* I'm glad we came here.

NICOLE. The food is good.

PAUL. I'm glad we came here, Nicole, on this trip together. *(Beat.)*

I saw a good movie. I went to the movies while you — It was one of their national, uh, directors. It was about a strike, in a textile factory, and the woman who leads it is in love with a hockey player who's going to be in the Olympics ... he was a goalie ... only he was gay ... and she had a sister who wanted to be in the army and was always drilling with a rifle, and cleaning the rifle, but it went off accidentally and killed one of the bosses at the factory, and then the other bosses had dinner together, and had a big spread, you know, a big ham *and* a turkey, and butlers ... and then there was a big riot ... and the hockey player got married. And then I thought maybe I didn't understand the part about him being gay, or got that wrong ... there were no subtitles, uh, in the film ... I think there was a symbolic, uh, element to the hockey or the locker room or, anyway, they boycotted the Olympics so the hockey players could stand on the picket lines, and I just, I *left*, basically, at that point because I was bored and I wanted to find you ... So we could have dinner. And I'm glad, I'm just glad you came back to the hotel in time for dinner. *(Beat.)* How was your tour?

NICOLE. All right.

PAUL. Yeah? Good. It all worked out? You just called, and you spoke to ...

NICOLE. Yep.

PAUL. The man at the airport?

NICOLE. That's the one.

PAUL. English?

NICOLE. No, native.

PAUL. He spoke English?

NICOLE. Very good English. Took me all around.

PAUL. Just you?

NICOLE. Yes.

PAUL. I guess I missed out.

NICOLE. I guess. *(Beat.)* It was a very good tour. It's a beautiful city.

PAUL. Yes. Good. The guide was good?

NICOLE. Very good. *(Beat.)*

PAUL. He and you — just the two of you?

NICOLE. Yes.

PAUL. Not very economical, for them.

NICOLE. It turned out to be.

PAUL. What do you mean? *(Beat.)*

NICOLE. We can't go back tomorrow.

PAUL. What?

NICOLE. I'm sorry. It's my fault, Paul. I don't know how to tell you this.

PAUL. What do you mean? Nicole, what happened?

NICOLE. Paul, this guide, the man I met. He ... You are not going to like this.

PAUL. *Nicole?*

NICOLE. I am so sorry. *(Beat.)* He took the passports.

PAUL. What?

NICOLE. And my money, and the tickets ...

PAUL. He robbed you?

NICOLE. Yes.

PAUL. Jesus Christ Nicole were you hurt? Are you all right, honey? *Did he hurt you?* What happened? He didn't hurt you, did he?

NICOLE. No, no ...

PAUL. My God did you notify the police?

NICOLE. Not yet.

PAUL. Not yet? We need to catch this guy. We need to call the embassy. We have to notify the airline. Why didn't you tell me this?

NICOLE. I'm sorry. I was so shocked.

PAUL. Do you know his name? Do you know anything about this guy?

NICOLE. No, no.

PAUL. How did it happen? Did he grab you, or —

NICOLE. No, he just ...

PAUL. Are you sure he didn't hurt you? Tell me!

NICOLE. Yes, I'm fine, I ... I don't know, I noticed they were gone at the end of the ... at a certain point, I guess, when I wasn't looking ...

PAUL. Just hold on. Hey. Slow down. Tell me exactly what happened. Okay?

NICOLE. We were on the tour. He was showing me around the city ...

PAUL. Yeah.

NICOLE. We stopped for a minute. We stopped to rest.

PAUL. Where?

NICOLE. Near the river. At this place he knew.

PAUL. When?

NICOLE. Just before I came to meet you, Paul.

PAUL. What kind of "place"?

NICOLE. Just a place. I guess I fell asleep.

PAUL. You fell asleep?

NICOLE. I was tired. It's been a long ...

PAUL. What kind of place was this where you could fall asleep?

NICOLE. Don't yell at me, Paul, for Chrissake, I'm sorry! I didn't mean to do it! It was just a place like on a bench in a park where it was quiet and we were resting and I must have fallen asleep for a second and when I woke up ...

PAUL. Yes?

NICOLE. When I woke up he was gone ...

PAUL. Oh, God.

NICOLE. And everything was gone, the money, tickets, passports ...

PAUL. Shit, goddamn it.

NICOLE. I'm sorry. *(Beat. She weeps. Beat.)*

PAUL. Thank God you weren't hurt.

NICOLE. I know you must be furious.

PAUL. I'm not.

NICOLE. You're not?

PAUL. I'm thankful nothing else happened to you.

NICOLE. You are?

PAUL. Yes, Nicole, yes, of course.

NICOLE. Even if we can't go home?

PAUL. We'll call the airlines and the embassy right after dinner, I'm sure we can work something out. If we have to stay for an extra day who cares? As long as you're all right.

NICOLE. I'm all right. I want to go home.

PAUL. So do I. You do?

NICOLE. Yes.

PAUL. Because earlier, you said —

NICOLE. When?

PAUL. When it was raining, you said —

NICOLE. I was wet, I was hungry —

PAUL. I was too. I was really cranky, and —

NICOLE. It's fine. It's fine.

PAUL. No, it's not, I was awful, and I'm sorry. I got so worried after you ran off.

NICOLE. What about?

PAUL. What about? Losing you. Having to find you. Being apart from you on our last day, when we only had a few more hours here together. And now, knowing that you weren't safe, that you had this trouble, I feel terrible, Nicole.

NICOLE. It's not your fault.

PAUL. It is and I feel awful and I love you, Nicole, I love you and I am so glad that you're all right.

NICOLE. I love you too.

PAUL. And I'm glad we were here together.

NICOLE. I'm sorry if we have to stay another day.

PAUL. I don't care as long as I'm with you.

NICOLE. We'll get home.

PAUL. Yes, we'll make it home okay, I promise, we'll get everything straightened out ... *(Beat.)* And you're right.

NICOLE. What?

PAUL. I don't know what I was thinking. The time. The earth ... you're totally right. When you fly over, it throws you ahead.

NICOLE. Oh ... Yes.

PAUL. But going back, going home, you're really going *back* — and it all reverses to put you back where you were before you left.

NICOLE. Yes. You sleep on the plane.

PAUL. Yes.

NICOLE. And then it's nine o'clock in the morning and you're home and wide awake.

End

NEW PLAYS

★ **INTIMATE APPAREL by Lynn Nottage.** The moving and lyrical story of a turn-of-the-century black seamstress whose gifted hands and sewing machine are the tools she uses to fashion her dreams from the whole cloth of her life's experiences. "...Nottage's play has a delicacy and eloquence that seem absolutely right for the time she is depicting..." *–NY Daily News.* "...thoughtful, affecting...The play offers poignant commentary on an era when the cut and color of one's dress—and of course, skin—determined whom one could and could not marry, sleep with, even talk to in public." *–Variety.* [2M, 4W] ISBN: 0-8222-2009-1

★ **BROOKLYN BOY by Donald Margulies.** A witty and insightful look at what happens to a writer when his novel hits the bestseller list. "The characters are beautifully drawn, the dialogue sparkles..." *–nytheatre.com.* "Few playwrights have the mastery to smartly investigate so much through a laugh-out-loud comedy that combines the vintage subject matter of successful writer-returning-to-ethnic-roots with the familiar mid-life crisis." *–Show Business Weekly.* [4M, 3W] ISBN: 0-8222-2074-1

★ **CROWNS by Regina Taylor.** Hats become a springboard for an exploration of black history and identity in this celebratory musical play. "Taylor pulls off a Hat Trick: She scores thrice, turning CROWNS into an artful amalgamation of oral history, fashion show, and musical theater..." *–TheatreMania.com.* "...wholly theatrical...Ms. Taylor has created a show that seems to arise out of spontaneous combustion, as if a bevy of department-store customers simultaneously decided to stage a revival meeting in the changing room." *–NY Times.* [1M, 6W (2 musicians)] ISBN: 0-8222-1963-8

★ **EXITS AND ENTRANCES by Athol Fugard.** The story of a relationship between a young playwright on the threshold of his career and an aging actor who has reached the end of his. "[Fugard] can say more with a single line than most playwrights convey in an entire script...Paraphrasing the title, it's safe to say this drama, making its memorable entrance into our consciousness, is unlikely to exit as long as a theater exists for exceptional work." *–Variety.* "A thought-provoking, elegant and engrossing new play..." *–Hollywood Reporter.* [2M] ISBN: 0-8222-2041-5

★ **BUG by Tracy Letts.** A thriller featuring a pair of star-crossed lovers in an Oklahoma City motel facing a bug invasion, paranoia, conspiracy theories and twisted psychological motives. "...obscenely exciting...top-flight craftsmanship. Buckle up and brace yourself..." *–NY Times.* "...[a] thoroughly outrageous and thoroughly entertaining play...the possibility of enemies, real and imagined, to squash has never been more theatrical." *–A.P.* [3M, 2W] ISBN: 0-8222-2016-4

★ **THOM PAIN (BASED ON NOTHING) by Will Eno.** An ordinary man muses on childhood, yearning, disappointment and loss, as he draws the audience into his last-ditch plea for empathy and enlightenment. "It's one of those treasured nights in the theater—treasured nights anywhere, for that matter—that can leave you both breathless with exhilaration and...in a puddle of tears." *–NY Times.* "Eno's words...are familiar, but proffered in a way that is constantly contradictory to our expectations. Beckett is certainly among his literary ancestors." *–nytheatre.com.* [1M] ISBN: 0-8222-2076-8

★ **THE LONG CHRISTMAS RIDE HOME by Paula Vogel.** Past, present and future collide on a snowy Christmas Eve for a troubled family of five. "...[a] lovely and hauntingly original family drama...a work that breathes so much life into the theater." *–Time Out.* "...[a] delicate visual feast..." *–NY Times.* "...brutal and lovely...the overall effect is magical." *–NY Newsday.* [3M, 3W] ISBN: 0-8222-2003-2

DRAMATISTS PLAY SERVICE, INC.
440 Park Avenue South, New York, NY 10016 212-683-8960 Fax 212-213-1539
postmaster@dramatists.com www.dramatists.com